D0647024

The
Victorian
Kitchen
Garden

A SEASONAL COMPANION

The Victorian Kitchen Garden

A SEASONAL COMPANION

COMPILED AND EDITED
BY JAN HUGHES

TEN SPEED PRESS
BERKELEY, CALIFORNIA

Copyright © 1996 by Ten Speed Press

A Kirsty Melville book

Ten Speed Press
P.O. Box 7123
Berkeley, CA 94707

Distributed in Australia by E.J. Dwyer Pty Ltd; in Canada by Publishers
Group West; in New Zealand by Tandem Press; in South Africa by Real
Books; and in the United Kingdom and Europe by Airlift Books.

Front cover image: courtesy of the Nursery Catalogue Collection,
Department of Special Collections, University of California, Davis
Back cover image: copyright Advance Seed Company
Interior and cover design by Randall Homan, Gestalt Graphics
Calligraphy by Tracey Hughes
Printed in Korea

ISBN 0-89815-798-6

1 2 3 4 5—99 98 97 96

INTRODUCTION

When Sir Walter Scott wrote "Nothing is more completely the child of art than the garden," he spoke to generations of Victorians who lovingly cultivated gardens for the purposes of contemplation, health, and beauty. The decorative motifs of flowers, fruit, and vegetables are today synonymous with the Victorian era, the influence of which extended beyond Queen Victoria's reign. Yet the Victorian gardener was also preoccupied with sustenance and the practical benefits of gardening. Nowhere was this more evident than in the kitchen garden where the fruits of labor could easily be transferred to the table.

The Victorian Kitchen Garden: A Seasonal Companion celebrates a year in the Victorian kitchen garden, from the cold winter months set aside for planning and cultivating, to spring, when the first new flowers and tender vegetables arrive, to summer with its bounty of fresh ripened fruit and blooming flowers, to fall with its abundant harvest of fruit and vegetables. Accompanying the wit, wisdom, and practical advice of writers of the day are the incredibly imaginative and delightful nursery seed catalogs, seed packages, advertisements, cards, and paintings of the time, many of which have never been published before.

In putting this book together, we came to the conclusion that the lost arts and lore of our great-grandparents have as much relevance today as they did a century ago. We hope that through these pages you will rediscover the spirit, humor, and charm of Victorian kitchen gardeners and perhaps adopt a little of their advice for yourself.

F. Barteldes & Co.

SEED CATALOGUE

1900

LAWRENCE, KANSAS.

JANUARY

IF IN JANUARY THE SUN DOTH MUCH APPEAR
MARCH AND APRIL WILL PAY FULL DEAR.

January
ADVICE

Flower Garden

In the outside flower garden little can be done except that shrubs may be pruned, or new work, such as making walks or grading, if weather permits.

Fruit Garden

Pruning, staking up, or mulching, can be done if the weather is such that the workman can stand out. No plant is injured by being pruned in cold weather, though the pruner may be.

Vegetable Garden

Nothing can be done this month in the northern states except to prepare manure, and get sashes, tools, etc. in working order, but in sections of the country where there is but little or no frost, the hardier kinds of seeds and plants may be sown and planted, such as asparagus, cabbage, cauliflower, carrot, leek, lettuce, onion, parsnip, peas, spinach, turnip, etc., etc. In any section where these seeds can be sown in the open ground, it is an indication that hotbeds may be begun for the sowing of such tender vegetables as tomatoes, egg and pepper plants, etc., though unless in the extreme southern states, hotbeds had better not be started before the first of February.

—PETER HENDERSON, *GARDENING FOR PLEASURE*

JANUARY

Welcome New Year!

What scenes are hidden in thy coming hours!
We greet thee with mingled joy and fear,
Knowing thou hast for us both thorn and flowers,
And as we blindly meet each newborn day,
We ask for guidance o'er the untried way.

—LADIES' HOME JOURNAL

SUCCESS WITH THE GARDEN

 How to Plan the Kitchen Garden

No matter how good a garden you had last year, you can have a better one this year. There is only one sure way: *Plan it in January as thoroughly as you would plan a house.*

- Send postal cards to all the seedsmen whose advertisements attract you. Get their catalogues.
- Measure accurately the length and breadth of your kitchen garden.
- Draw a diagram of it to scale.
- Then decide which way to run the rows.
- Decide how much space you can give to the things that require a lot of room—corn, potatoes, cabbages, and vines of the cucumber family.
- Then make a line for every single row of vegetables and name each crop.
- Then plan your succession of crops.

—THE EDITORS, *THE GARDEN MAGAZINE*

BAKED WINTER SQUASH

Cut open the squash, take out the seeds and without paring cut it up into large pieces; put the pieces in tins or in a dripping pan, place in a moderately hot oven and bake about an hour. When done, peel and mash like mashed potatoes, or serve the pieces hot on a dish, to be eaten warm with butter. It retains its sweetness much better baked this way than when boiled.

—MRS. F. L. GILLETTE, *THE WHITE HOUSE COOK BOOK*

 All my hurts, my garden spade can heal. —RALPH WALDO EMERSON

garden may begin in the spring
1 the earliest vegetables, or it may
1n in the mind with the vegetables
which there is the greatest affection.

—EDITH L. FULLERTON,
HOW TO MAKE A VEGETABLE GARDEN

VHAT OUR SEEDS
WILL DO FOR YOU.

◇———◆———◇

The First Year of Gardening

you are a beginner in gardening
d this is your first garden, don't
ad in fevered haste every garden
ok you can lay your hands on.
the multitude of counsel there
ay sometimes be safety, but
ere is oftener confusion. It is
tter to take one good authority
d stick to him, for your first
ar's gardening at least. Don't
an a larger garden than you can
anage comfortably. Don't try
y but easily-grown plants: the
d and inexpensive sorts are the
ost satisfactory, after all.

—FRANCES DUNCAN, *LADIES' HOME JOURNAL*

◇———◆———◇

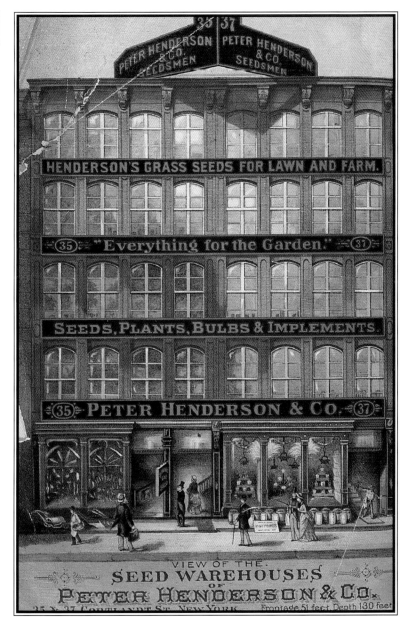

VIEW OF THE
SEED WAREHOUSES
OF
PETER HENDERSON & CO.
35 & 37 CORTLANDT ST., NEW YORK. Frontage 51 feet, Depth 130 feet

Order catalogues now;
it is not too early to
plan your garden and
place orders for seeds.

Salubrious Celery

Celery is one of the very best things to have in the garden, for it is one of the tonic vegetables, coming to us when greens are scarce, and when the physique that craves meat, and is eating much of it, finds in celery the needed counterbalance. It is considered the best nerve tonic in existence, and many people are so fond of it they carry the dried root in the pocket, chewing it as children chew gum.

—EDITH L. FULLERTON,
HOW TO MAKE A VEGETABLE GARDEN

Wash celery carefully and put in cold water to keep crisp till dinner. Remove all the green, as nothing is so ornamental as the pure white leaves of bleached celery. If the ends of the stalks have been broken, split and curl them.

—MRS. S. T., IN M. C. TYREE,
HOUSEKEEPING IN OLD VIRGINIA

Celery may be sown any time from Christmas to April.

Few soups are perfect in which celery or celery seed has not been used as flavoring.

—BEETON'S NEW DICTIONARY OF EVERY-DAY GARDENING

✦ CELERY SOUP ✦

Cut down the white of a half a dozen heads of celery into little pieces and boil in four quarts of white stock, with a quarter pound of lean ham and two ounces of butter. Simmer gently for a full hour, then strain through a sieve, return the liquor to the pan, and stir in a few spoonfuls of cream with great care. Serve with toasted bread, and, if liked, thicken with a little flour. Season to taste.

—MRS. F. L. GILLETTE, *THE WHITE HOUSE COOK BOOK*

Does a garden pay? As I look at it, you might as well ask, Does a sunset pay?

—CHARLES DUDLEY WARNER, *MY SUMMER IN A GARDEN*

SEEDS

WATER MELON
DIXIE

BURT'S SEED FOR QUALITY

CHRYSANTHEMUM
BEST MIXED

BURT'S SEED FOR QUALITY

A seed we say is a simple thing,
The germ of a flower or weed—
But all the Earth's workmen, laboring
With all the help that wealth could bring,
Never could make a seed.

—JULIAN S. CUTLER, AS QUOTED IN *DE GARDENNE BOKE*

There is a saying in the countryside that to raise a crop of turnips you must begin by having only half enough seed, must give away part of it, fall and spill half you have left, then sow the balance. The moral is, of course, against sowing too thickly such things as can not be handily thinned…Sow enough, but not too much, seed in fine, light ground, and be sure not to cover your sowings with more than twice the seed-depth…Very fine seed would be better mixed with dust or ashes before sowing. Put bulky ones in holes made with the fore-finger and press the earth well over each.

—MARTHA MCCULLOCH WILLIAMS,
THE DELINEATOR

BEANS
KENTUCKY WONDER

Storing Kitchen Garden Seeds: Whether seeds are saved or bought, great car must be taken in storing them. is not well to commit the seeds to boxes and drawers; the safest plan is to hang them up in smal paper or muslin bags. Peas and beans, which are subject to mag gots, should be looked over occ sionally and kept clean. Seeds o some sorts of vegetables will ke good for years; but, of course, is best to use new seeds; for ol seed, when good, does not germ nate as quickly as new.

—BEETON'S DICTIONARY
OF EVERY-DAY GARDENING

General List of VEGETABLE SEEDS

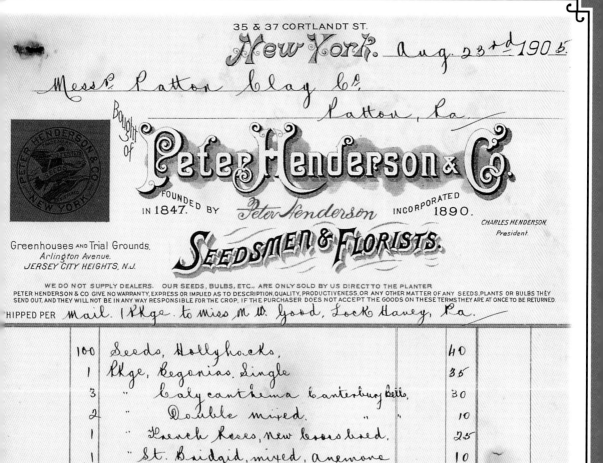

The Law of Colors in Flowers
or Buyer Beware

Not a season passes but some…swindling dealers have the audacity to plant themselves right in the business centers of our large cities, and hundreds of our sharp business men glide smoothly into their nets. The very men who will chuckle at the misfortunes of a poor rustic when he falls into the hands of a mock auctioneer, or a pocket-book dropper, will freely pay ten dollars for a rose plant of which a picture has been shown them as having a blue flower; the chance of its coming blue being about equal to the chance that the watch of the mock auctioneer will be gold. It has long been known among the best observers of such matters, that in certain families of plants, particular colors will prevail, and that in no single instance can we ever expect to see *blue, yellow* and *scarlet* colors in varieties of the same species. If any one at all conversant with plants will bring any family of them to mind, it will at once be seen how undeviating is this law.

—PETER HENDERSON, *GARDENING FOR PLEASURE*

If you were buying cows, horses, or chickens, you would be careful to see that they had been bred from fine, healthy stock. Why should you not be as careful in the selection of your seeds?

—EDITH L. FULLERTON, *HOW TO MAKE A VEGETABLE GARDEN*

Quarter Century
Offering of
NORTHRUP KING & CO'S
Sterling
Seeds.

1909

INEXPERIENCE

N. K & CO'S
STERLING
SEEDS
RECLEANED

EXAGGERATION

CARELESSNESS

IGNORANCE

Of Importance to Seed Buyers

THERE IS NO BUSINESS IN THE WORLD IN WHICH
KNOWLEDGE AND **EXPERIENCE** ON THE PART OF THE SELLER
MEAN SO MUCH TO THE **BUYER** AS IN THE **SEED BUSINESS.**

COUPLED WITH A WELL-SETTLED CONVICTION OF THE PRINCIPLES
ON WHICH A SEED BUSINESS SHOULD BE CONDUCTED, THE EXERCISE
OF THESE QUALIFICATIONS AFFORDS THE GREATEST PROTECTION
THE PURCHASER HAS AGAINST DISAPPOINTMENT AND LOSS.

MANY YEARS DEVOTED TO THE GROWTH AND SALE OF SEEDS,
HAVE GIVEN US A KNOWLEDGE OF THE BEST VARIETIES.

THAT KNOWLEDGE WE PLACE AT THE SERVICE OF SEED
BUYERS IN THE PAGES WHICH FOLLOW.

NORTHRUP, KING & CO

SEEDSMEN, MINNEAPOLIS, MINNESOTA.

FEBRUARY

CANDLEMAS DAY, PLANT BEANS IN THE CLAY
PUT CANDLES AND CANDLESTICKS AWAY.

February
ADVICE

Flower Garden

The directions for January will in the main apply to this month, except that now some of the hardier annuals may be sown, and also the propagation of plants by cuttings may be done rather better now than in January.

Fruit Garden

But little can be done in most of the northern states as yet, and in sections where there is no frost on the ground, it is likely to be too wet to work; but in many southern states this will be the best month for planting fruit trees and plants of all kinds, particularly strawberries, raspberries, blackberries, pear and apple, while grape-vines do better a month later...

LOVING ❤ GREETING

Vegetable Garden

Horse manure, leaves from the woods, or any refuse hops from the breweries, when they can be obtained, may be got together towards the latter part of the month and mixed and turned to get "sweetened" preparatory to forming hotbeds. Manure that is to be used for the crops should be turned and broken up as fine as possible, for it should be known that the more completely manure of any kind can be mixed with the soil, the better will be the crop.

—PETER HENDERSON, *GARDENING FOR PLEASURE*

FEBRUARY

Forget-Me-Not

Sweet fragile weed, while thus I view
Thy softened tint of constant blue,
I pray in life whate'er my lot
May those I love Forget-me-not.

—MARY PIRIE, *A POPULAR BOOK ON FLOWERS, GRASSES, AND SHRUBS*

To remember your Birthday.

I congratulate, wish you well and rejoice that fortune which gave you birth also gave me in you a friend.

With love and best wishes

Mrs B. W. King

The flower symbolizes
constancy, and is
traditionally exchanged
by friends on February 29.

Winter Vegetables

The winter supply of vegetables is drawn largely from root crops. And it is interesting to observe how, in order to meet the desire for the same flavors as the leaves give us in the summer time, there has been developed a multitude of bulbous equivalents for such things as parsley cabbage, etc. There is as rich a variety possible in the crops which we grow under the ground as in those which are above the surface.

—H. B. FULLERTON, *COUNTRY LIFE IN AMERICA*

TO BOIL BEETS

Wash them. Do not break or cut the roots. Leave an inch of the tops, so that the color and juice cannot escape. Boil hard for two hours. When tender, slice them, sprinkling over the sugar, then butter and salt to the taste. Sugar is the greatest improvement.

—MRS. S. T., IN M. C. TYREE, *HOUSEKEEPING IN OLD VIRGINIA*

COOKING ROOTS

As a rule, roots should be cooked in unsalted water. Salt hardens in water, and also toughens the wood fiber contained in the roots, rendering them not only more unpalatable, but more indigestible.

—EDITH L. FULLERTON, *HOW TO MAKE A VEGETABLE GARDEN*

Cauliflower is nothing but cabbage with a college education.

—MARK TWAIN

To Whiten Cauliflower

…uliflowers, more imperatively than cabbage, demand …nty of water and weather not too hot. When they …in to head, the large leaves should be bent over the …er part to whiten it.

—L. H. BAILEY, *GARDEN-MAKING*

Growing Broccoli

…early use, sow in February, and transplant in spring. …fall use, sow in spring in drills, and transplant in …y, in deep, rich soil, two feet apart each way; culti-…e same as Cabbage. An ounce [of seed] will produce …e thousand plants.

—*SHAKER SEED CATALOGUE*

…occoli is in some respects superior to cauliflower, …ich it very much resembles. The early varieties with-…nd drought and ill usage better than cauliflower, and …, on that account, easier for the amateur to grow.

—L. H. BAILEY, *GARDEN-MAKING*

Root crops such as carrots, onions, potatoes, and turnips grow deeper if the coming winter will be severe.

 WINTER SALAD

Cut raw well-bleached Winter Chicory leaves as thin as possible and mix with hot beetroot for a winter salad.

—MRS. CAMERON LUCY, *HEARTS AND SPADES*

FEBRUARY ~LORE~

St. Valentine's Day is good for sowing peas, lettuce, sweet peas, and cabbage in gardens in warmer climates.

Valentine's Divination: If on Valentine's eve, you write the names of any would-be lovers on bits of paper, roll them into clay balls and drop them into a bowl of water before you go to bed, the one that rises to the top by morning will be your Valentine.

—TRADITIONAL

TOOL LORE

Rowan tree and red thread
Hold the witches all in dread.

〜 Witches are said to dislike the wood of an ash tree, also known as rowan tree. An iron tool with an ashwood handle promises security for its owner. Planted in the garden, it protects the family, the house and the crop against evil.

For if in your house a man shoulders a spade,
For you and your kinfolk a grave is half made.

〜 Any sharp tool, such as a hoe or a spade, brought into the house, will "cut" the household's good fortune in half, and must be immediately taken outside by the same door through which it came in. Similarly, if you give a sharp tool as a present to a gardener, he or she must "buy" it from you, or your friendship could be "severed."

〜 To lay a rake on the ground with its teeth upright will bring bad luck, a poor crop, or rain. To safeguard against any ill influences, one must curtsy to the sun in apology as the tool is picked up.

〜 Never lay tools across each other on the ground, or bad luck could "cross" your path.

—TRADITIONAL

I n February: Tools can now be inspected and repaired, and any new ones that are needed made or ordered.

—L. H. BAILEY, *GARDEN-MAKING*

HOEING

As I drew still fresher soil about the rows with my ho[e] I disturbed the ashes of unchronicled nations who in primeval years lived under these heavens, and their small implements of war and hunting were brought to life by this modern day…When my hoe tinkled agains[t] the stones, that music echoed to the woods and the sk[y] and was an accompaniment to my labor which yielded an instant and immeasurable crop.

—HENRY DAVID THOREAU, *WALDEN*

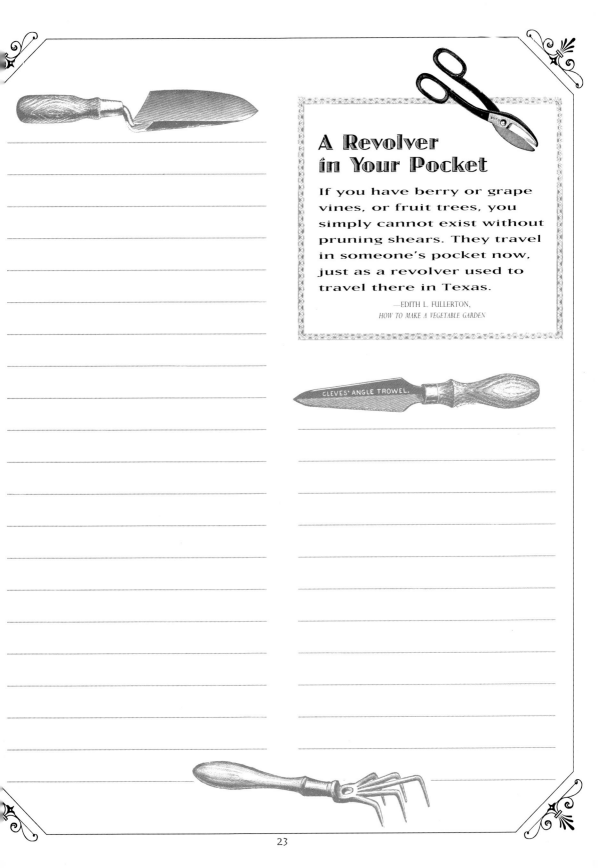

A Revolver in Your Pocket

If you have berry or grape vines, or fruit trees, you simply cannot exist without pruning shears. They travel in someone's pocket now, just as a revolver used to travel there in Texas.

—EDITH L. FULLERTON,
HOW TO MAKE A VEGETABLE GARDEN

CLEVES' ANGLE TROWEL.

RECIPES

Good seeds are cheap at any price.

—MARTHA MCCULLOCH WILLIAMS, *THE DELINEATOR*

MARCH

SO MANY FROSTS IN MARCH,
SO MANY IN MAY.

March
ADVICE

Fruit Garden

In light, dry soils, planting may be safely done in many sections, but we again caution the inexperienced not to get impatient and begin to plant before the ground is dry; it is bad to do so even in light sandy soils, but in stiff and clayey ones it will be utter destruction. Again at this season, although a tree or plant will receive no injury when its roots are in the soil, should a frost come during planting, yet that same amount of freezing would greatly injure the plant if the roots were uncovered and exposed.

Vegetable Garden

This is a busy month. Hotbeds must be now all started, and all the seeds of the hardier vegetables may be sown in locations where the frost is out and the ground dry; the list given for January may now be used at the north, while for most of the southern states the tender kinds of vegetables may now be sown and planted, such as eggplant, okra, melon, sweet potatoes, squash, tomatoes, etc.

—PETER HENDERSON, *GARDENING FOR PLEASURE*

Tidying Up

March is the month when a garden form of "spring house-cleaning" is in order. Roses are still in their straw jackets and the plants in garden beds and borders are still asleep, their feet snugly covered by winter blankets of stable-litter or leaves. As soon as the weather permits, this covering should be removed. If the "blanket" of mulch is kept on too long, the plants, becoming overheated, start to grow, and when the covering is removed, finding chilly April weather when they had expected that of late May, they take cold as easily as incubator chicks or children kept in overheated rooms.

—FRANCES DUNCAN, *LADIES' HOME JOURNAL*

MARCH

It is the first mild day of March:
Each minute sweeter than before,
The redbreast sings from the tall larch
That stands beside our door.

—WILLIAM WORDSWORTH, *TO MY SISTER*

No one sends a baby out into all weathers just because at a certain calendar date spring is supposed to have come, and gardeners treat infant plants with the same care.

—FRANCES DUNCAN, *LADIES' HOME JOURNAL*

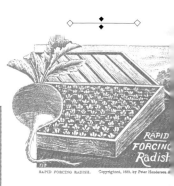

RAPID FORCING Radish

RAPID FORCING RADISH. Copyrighted, 1889, by Peter Henderson

GENERAL LIST of VEGETABLE SEEDS

100-YEARS OLD RECIPE

TO KEEP ASPARAGUS ALL YEAR

Boil the Asparagus very lightly, then take them out of the water. Put them in a dish till quite dry, then place them in a jar or pot and cover them with clarified butter. Tie the top of the pot very tightly and set in a cool place. In a month clarify the butter again, and it will keep a year.

—MRS. CAMERON LUCY, *HEARTS AND SPADES*

Plant Asparagus in March

Asparagus plants may be sown from seed, but it is easier and cheaper to buy them for small gardens. Good strong two- or three-year-old plants should be set in wide open furrows six inches deep, three feet apart in the rows, with rows five feet apart. The furrows are then filled in slowly during summer cultivation, till the surface is entirely level. For the first two or three years, and occasionally thereafter, a heavy dressing of well-rotted manure should be worked into the surface in spring…It is not advisable to cut the bed until the plants are three years set, and the cutting should always cease in June or by the first of July. In the fall all the old canes should be cut back and burned.

—L. H. BAILEY, *GARDEN-MAKING*

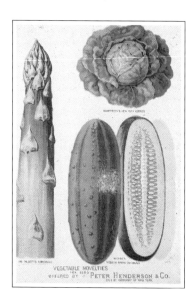

VEGETABLE NOVELTIES
FOR 1883
OFFERED BY PETER HENDERSON & Co.

The Hotbed

A Hotbed consists of a wooden frame, generally six feet wide, and from six to sixteen feet long…The frame should face the south or south-east. After completion, place it on a manure bed, prepared in the following manner: fill in about ten inches of rich, pulverized soil, and allow it to stand for a few days, giving it air by slightly raising the sashes, so that the fiery vapor, or steam, may escape. The seeds of cabbages, cauliflowers, peppers, tomatoes, and other hardy varieties may be sown, and the plants planted out as soon as the weather begins to be warm.

—D. M. FERRY DESCRIPTIVE CATALOGUE

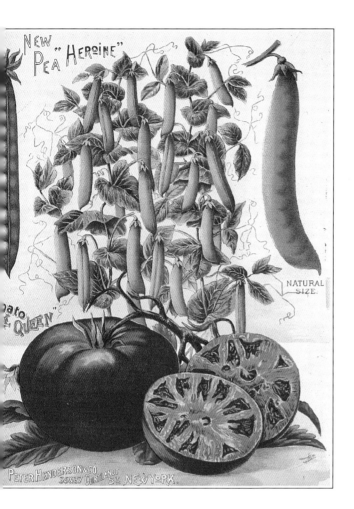

NEW PEA "HEROINE"

NATURAL SIZE.

"Potato "QUEEN"

PETER HENDERSON & CO. 35&37 CORTLANDT ST. NEW YORK.

◁ Intercropping Peas ▷

[ins]tead of devoting a portion of the garden to peas alone, as is usually [do]ne, plant them in single lines amongst other crops: the plants will [thu]s get more sun and air, and bear much longer and more abundantly.

—BEETON'S DICTIONARY OF EVERY-DAY GARDENING

◁ Cultivation of the Pea ▷

[Th]e seed can be planted in March, to avoid the spring rush. It germi[nat]es rapidly, runs in a short space of time, blossoms in profusion and [sho]ws an exquisite flower. Extra-early peas should be planted as soon [as] the ground can be thoroughly worked. As the support is to be [pla]ced between the two furrows, make them four inches deep and six [inc]hes apart, if the vines are to climb on brush; or four inches apart if [the]y are to climb on a portable wire fence.

—EDITH L. FULLERTON, COUNTRY LIFE IN AMERICA

MARCH ～LORE～

Eat leeks in March and ransoms [wild garlic] in May, And all the year after physicians may play.

～ Sow sweet peas on St. Patrick's Day for more fragrant blossoms.

～ Plant cabbage on St. Patrick's Day: for the best results, the work must be done before dawn.

～ If the first three days of March are not cold and windy, stormy weather will come in the "Borrowing Days" of the month's end.

～ Indigenous trees will let the gardener know when the threat of the last frost has passed—they will put out their leaves.

—TRADITIONAL

I f the housewife is also the gardener, she is
sure to put some new life into her garden,
for what is more satisfactory than being able
to offer the family an entirely new dish.

—EDITH L. FULLERTON, *HOW TO MAKE A VEGETABLE GARDEN*

Woman's Work

No one will deny that gardening is a very healthy form of exercise, nor will any girl who cares about her garden go out in the listless, uninterested manner of the girl who has no such inducement, who is in no hurry to go out because she has nothing to do when she gets there. The result of having varied occupations in view will be that the girl will be eager to go out, and happy and busy during the whole time of her recreation. Then comes the pleasure she will have in the flowers when grown. There is another kind of pleasure which she will also derive from gardening if she only sets her mind to it, and that is the pleasure of giving.

—H. R. VERNON, *ATLANTA*

THE GARDEN-WIFE

arden-wives are the most fashionable form of Mutual Admiration Society, though their method of express- their appreciation is somewhat primitive, and recalls habits of the Mendicant Orders of the middle ages Two garden-wives meeting always start with a chorus admiration about gardens in general, during which one s with the other in rolling out Latin names with ally the wrong terminations. They then descend to ticulars of roots and bulbs, and the chorus ends by one ding the other come over and see her own special den, particularly her herbaceous border.

h yes, I look after it entirely myself. Of course I get gardener to weed it, and manure it, and to do all se tiresome dirty sort of things that merely break 's back, and of course when I am working in it, garden boy has to come and clear up after me, except for that I do it entirely myself, entirely."

ere are some garden-wives with whom one is acquainted, o not only possess considerable practical knowledge, d that mysterious attribute "the gardener's thumb," who also leave a dainty footprint, if not upon the ds of time, at least upon the good brown earth of ir garden.

—THE HONORABLE MRS. ANSTRUTHER, *CORNHILL MAGAZINE*

MOON  FARMING

I n the new of the moon is the time to set hens, to plant corn and other things that grow above ground. Planted in the old of the moon, seeds of such plants will probably rot. On the other hand, crops that grow under the ground, as potatoes and beets, should be planted in the old of the moon; and plants that tend to run too much vine and straw should be planted at this period. Beans planted when the moon is on the wane will not cling to their poles. Grain purchased in the full of the moon will be of full weight…The moon foreshadows the changes in the weather. It chills and injures plants on clear nights. In the full, it causes wounds to heal…When certain constellations reign, the sign is in the head or in the feet; and then wizards know what is to transpire when the crops are planted.

—L. H. BAILEY, *THE INDEPENDENT*

> **N** either sowing, planting, or grafting should ever be undertaken without scrupulous attention to the increase or waning of the moon.
>
> —SIR EDWARD TAYLOR, *PRIMITIVE CULTURE*

✦ Worldly Wisdom ✦

☞ Peas and beans planted during the increase of the moon will climb; planted in the wane, they cling to the ground. ☞ Peas will refuse to climb up last year's sticks, but beans won't mind. ☞ Plant peas in the morning to rise with the sun; plant tubers in the afternoon to sink with the sun. ☞ Plant and transplant flowers in the moonlight and plant cuttings at the August new moon. ☞ Plant trees in the waxing moon: *"From moon being changed, till past be the prime, for grafting and cropping is very good time."* ☞ Chives are under the dominion of Mars.

☞ Dill is under the dominion of Mercury, and therefore thought to strengthen the brain. ☞ Asparagus is ruled by Jupiter. ☞ Strawberries are ruled by Venus. ☞ Parsley and marjoram are governed by Mercury. ☞ Lettuce is governed by the moon. ☞ To rid your house of spiders, sweep it in the dark of the moon. ☞ It is good luck for the new moon to come on Monday, or "moon-day." ☞ To point to the new moon brings bad luck. ☞ A halo around the moon means rain. ☞ If thunder occurs during the moon's change, mild weather and good crops will follow. ☞ Potatoes planted on the new moon will be the size of peas.

"...But potatoes now, are a different thing. They want to grow down, that is plain, But don't ye see, you must plant for that, When the moon is on the wane!"

—TRADITIONAL

ANGEL OF MIDNIGHT FIELD CORN.

◁ Planting by the Moon ▷

The general rules of planting by the moon are: plant things that grow above the ground in new moon phases, and things which grow underground in old moon phases; be sure to plant when the moon is in the "fruitful" signs of Cancer, Scorpio, Pisces; if necessary, one can plant in the semi-fruitful signs of Taurus, Libra or Capricorn. Avoid planting in the barren signs of Leo, Aquarius, Aries, Gemini, or Sagittarius, as these signs are better for harvesting, weeding, destroying insects, and cultivating or turning sod.

—TRADITIONAL

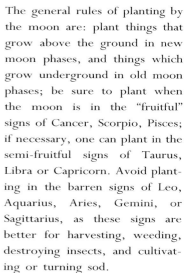

JANUARY	SNOW MOON
FEBRUARY	TRAPPER'S MOON
MARCH	WAKENING MOON
APRIL	GRASS MOON
MAY	PLANTING MOON
JUNE	ROSE MOON
JULY	SUMMER MOON
AUGUST	MAIZE MOON
SEPTEMBER	FALL MOON
OCTOBER	HARVEST MOON
NOVEMBER	MOON OF THE FALLING LEAVES
DECEMBER	CHRISTMAS MOON

◁ Canning by the Moon ▷

Canning is best done during a waning moon in the third or fourth quarter when the moon is in the watery signs of Scorpio, Cancer, or Pisces. Jellies and preserves can be made in the waning of the moon during the fixed signs of Aquarius, Taurus, Leo, or Scorpio.

—TRADITIONAL

WHEN APRIL BLOWS HIS HORN,
IT'S GOOD FOR HAY AND CORN.

April
ADVICE

Flower Gardens

The planting of all kinds of hardy herbaceous plants and shrubs may now be done in the flower garden. Bulbs and all tender plants that have been covered for protection in winter may now be stripped, and the beds lightly forked and raked. Sow tender annual flower seeds in boxes.

Fruit Gardens

Strawberries that have been covered up by straw or leaves, should now be relieved around the plant, only leaving the covering between the plants. Raspberries, grapevines, etc., that have been laid down may now be uncovered and tied up to stakes or trellises, and all new plantations of these and other fruits should now be made.

Vegetable Gardens

The hardier sorts of vegetable seeds and plants, such as beets, cabbage, cauliflower, celery, lettuce, onions, parsley, parsnip, peas, potatoes, radishes, spinach, turnip, etc., should all be sown or planted this month, if the soil is dry and warm…It is quite a common practice with many amateurs to delay garden operations of all kinds until May, but all the hardier sorts of vegetables are likely to be later and inferior in consequence.

—PETER HENDERSON, *GARDENING FOR PLEASURE*

APRIL

In the spring, although a young man's fancy may lightly turn in the direction which Tennyson suggested, the gardener has not time for any such diversion; it is his busy season.

—FRANCES DUNCAN, *LADIES' HOME JOURNAL*

HENDERSON'S BOUNTIFUL BEAN

❖ BEANS ❖

The ancients made use of beans in gathering the votes of the people, and for electing the magistrates. A white bean signifies absolution, and a black one, condemnation. From this practice, no doubt, was derived the p of black-balling, as it is called, obnoxious persons.

—JOHN L. BLAKE, D. D., *THE FARMER'S EVERYDAY BOOK*

What shall I learn of beans or beans of me? I cheri them, I hoe them, early and late I have an eye t them; and this is my day's work.

—HENRY DAVID THOREAU, *WALDEN*

The bean is a graceful, confiding, engaging vine; but you never can put beans into poetry, not into the highest sort of prose. The bean has no dignity.

—CHARLES DUDLEY WARNER, *MY SUMMER IN A GARDEN*

Culture of Beans

In outdoor culture the seed should not be sown until the middle of April in sunny spots, or in the beginning of May in positions not so open to the sun, and from this time crops may be sown in succession once a fortnight, or thereabouts, until the end of July. Plant in rows eighteen inches to two feet apart, and from nine to twelve inches apart in the rows.

—*BEETON'S NEW DICTIONARY OF EVERY-DAY GARDENING*

❖ Broadbeans planted in Leap Yea "grow backwards in the pod."

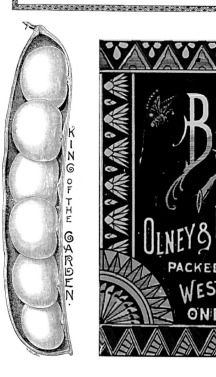

KING OF THE GARDEN.

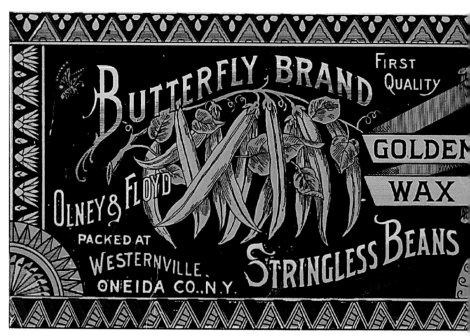

BUTTERFLY BRAND FIRST QUALITY

OLNEY & FLOYD

PACKED AT WESTERNVILLE, ONEIDA CO., N.Y.

GOLDEN WAX STRINGLESS BEANS

1899

He who ploughs land, spins gold.

❖ ❖ ❖ ❖

Food and Fable

The old Pythagorean theory was that the bean held the principle of human life; it was said to be the first food eaten by mankind; it was in a way sacred to Apollo; for the introduction into Europe of the haricot bean we are indebted to no less a person than Alexander the Great; the smell of beans in blossom is credited with all sorts of effects on minds and morals.

—WALTER RICHARDS, *THE LIVING AGE*

BRAND BEANS

...ERFLY

TRADE MARK

WESTERNVILLE N.Y.

...EY AND FLOYD

➳ WINTER VEGETABLE SOUP ➳

Scrape and slice three turnips and three carrots and peel three onions, and fry them all with a little butter until light yellow; add a bunch of celery and three or four leeks cut into pieces; stir and fry all the ingredients for six minutes; when fried, add one clove of garlic, two stalks of parsley, two cloves, salt, pepper and a little grated nutmeg; cover with three quarts of water and simmer for three hours, taking off the scum carefully. Croutons, vermicelli, Italian pastes, or rice may be added.

➳ SPRING VEGETABLE SOUP ➳

Half a pint of green peas, two shredded lettuces, one onion, a small bunch of parsley, two ounces of butter, the yolks of three eggs, one pint of water, and one and a half quarts of soup stock. Put in a stewpan the lettuce, onion, parsley, and butter, with one pint of water, and let them simmer until tender. Season with salt and pepper. When done, strain off the vegetables, and put two-thirds of the liquid with the stock. Beat up the yolks of the eggs with the other third, toss it over the fire, and at the moment of serving add this with the vegetables to the strained off soup.

—MRS. F. L. GILLETTE, *THE WHITE HOUSE COOK BOOK*

❖ ❖ ❖ ❖

A Man and His Garden

What a man needs in gardening is
a cast-iron back, with a hinge in it.

—CHARLES DUDLEY WARNER, *MY SUMMER IN A GARDEN*

Why a Man Should Have ✦ a Garden ✦

In all ages the garden has been an object of desire with kings and philosophers. No other sort of abode seems to contribute so much to the tranquillity of mind and rest of body. The sweetness of the air, the pleasantness of the smell, the verdure of the plants, the exercise of working and walking; but, above all, the exemption from care, seems equally to favor and improve both contemplation and health, enjoyment of sense and imagination, and thereby the quiet and ease of both body and mind. A poor man may not afford having a costly house, rich furniture, or an expensive carriage, but he can afford to have a garden.

—JOHN L. BLAKE, D. D.,
THE FARMER'S EVERYDAY BOOK

If the masculine portion of the family
has the garden in charge, it is his
bounden duty to give the housewife at
least one new vegetable each year.

—EDITH L. FULLERTON, *HOW TO MAKE A VEGETABLE GARDEN*

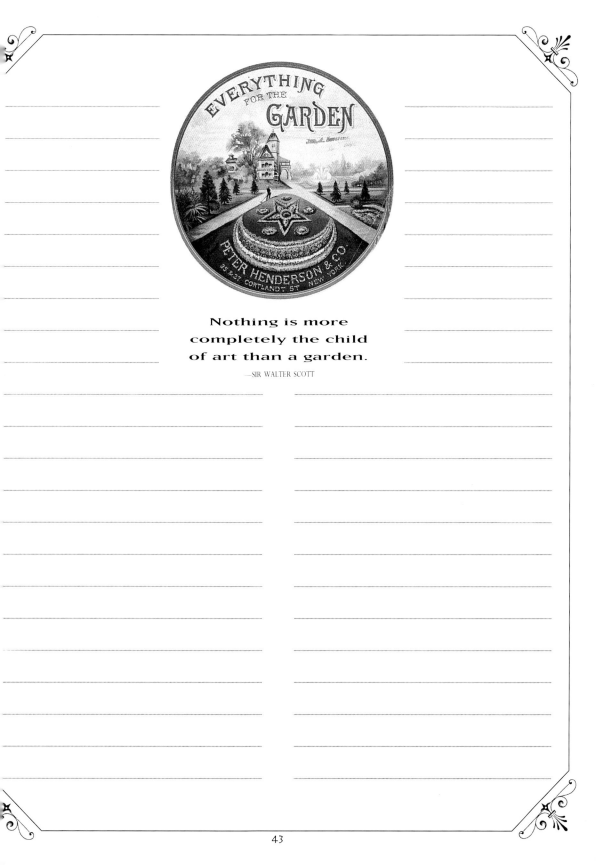

Nothing is more
completely the child
of art than a garden.

—SIR WALTER SCOTT

A PLAGUE OF LOCUSTS

(and Aphids and Dandelions and Caterpillars...)

> **S**oon I found that my lines had fallen in a place where vegetable growth had to run the gauntlet of as many foes and trials as a Christian pilgrim... On every leaf, and both sides of it, and at the root of everything that grew, was a professional specialist in the shape of a gnat, caterpillar, aphis, or other expert, whose business it was to devour that particular part, and help murder the whole attempt at vegetation.
>
> —OLIVER WENDELL HOLMES,
> AS QUOTED IN *DE GARDENNE BOKE*

Garden Unity

We must have sound and move ment besides color and beauty form if our gardens are to be complete. Nature will look afte it for us; we shall be put to no trouble: the pollen will be brou to the stigma, the bird will dev the insect; and we shall accept song, the flower, the fruit, with no very clear idea of the degree of our dependence.

—THE HONORABLE ALICIA AMHERST,
REVIEW OF REVIEWS

➤ Inexpensive Gardeners' Assistants ➤

Don't kill the harmless garter snake that slips across your path—he is on no errand of mischief, but one of beneficence. If Eve had set the serpent to work at his proper business of killing insects he would have had no leisure for temptation. Encourage the birds, especially the titmice, wrens, orioles, and woodpeckers, but above all invite the presence of toads.

—FRANCES DUNCAN, *LADIES' HOME JOURNAL*

Toads eat rose bugs and many other slugs and insect pests as eagerly as if they were the sweetest morsels in the world…If we had toads enough in the garden we could have more roses and more grapes.

—*THE OLD FARMER'S ALMANAC*

Feed your garden before it gets hungry, rest it before it's weary, and weed it before it gets foul.

—JOHN L. BLAKE, D. D.,
THE FARMER'S EVERYDAY BOOK

One year's seeding makes seven years weeding.

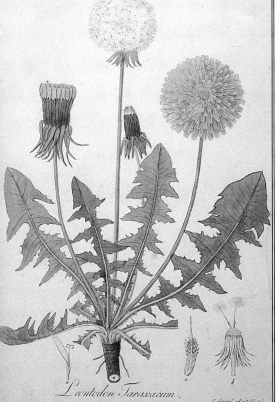

Leontodon Taraxacum.

I scarcely dare trust myself to speak of the weeds. They grow as if the devil was in them. I know a lady, a member of the church, and a very good sort of woman, considering the subject condition of that class, who says that the weeds work on her to that extent, in going through her garden, she has the greatest difficulty in keeping the ten commandments in anything like an unfractured condition. I asked her which one, but she said, all of them: one felt like breaking the whole lot.

—CHARLES DUDLEY WARNER, *MY SUMMER IN A GARDEN*

Weeds can be raised cheaper than most other crops, because they will bear more neglect.

—*THE OLD FARMER'S ALMANAC*

MAY

MIST IN MAY AND HEAT IN JUNE
BRING ALL THINGS INTO TUNE.

May
ADVICE

Flower Garden

If weeds are not kept down as they first appear, treble the labor will be required to eradicate them next month. Annuals that have

been sown in the greenhouse or hotbed may now be planted out, and seeds of such sorts as Mignonette, Sweet Alyssum, Phlox Drummondii, Portulaca, etc., etc., may be sown in the borders.

Fruit Garden

Where it has not been convenient before, most of the smaller fruits may yet be planted the first part of the month. Ply the hoe vigorously to keep down weeds. If any of the numerous varieties of caterpillars, slugs or worms make their appearance on the young shoots of vines or trees, a free application of tobacco dust will dislodge most of them. It is best to use it as a preventative, for if they once get a foothold, the crop may be ruined.

Vegetable Garden

Thin out all crops sown last month that are now large enough, and hoe deeply all planted crops such as cabbage, cauliflower, lettuce, etc. Plant out all tender vegetables, viz: tomatoes, egg and pepper plants, sweet potatoes, etc. Plant seeds of lima beans, corn, melons, okra, cucumbers, etc. and succession crops of peas spinach, lettuce, beans, etc.

—PETER HENDERSON,
GARDENING FOR PLEASURE

MAY

_____   _____

_____   _____

_____   _____

_____   _____

_____   _____

_____   _____

_____   _____

_____   _____

_____   _____

_____   _____

_____   _____

_____   _____

_____   _____

_____   _____

_____   _____

_____   _____

Flower in the crannied wall
I pluck you out of the crannies,
I hold you here, root and all, in my hand,
Little flower—but if I could understand
What you are, root and all, and all in all,
I should know what God and man is.

—ALFRED, LORD TENNYSON, *FLOWER IN THE CRANNIED WALL*

MAY LORE

Sow your cucumbers in March,
You will need neither bag nor sack;
Sow them in April, you will have a few;
I will sow mine in May,
And I will have more than you!

⁓ Plant your watermelons before sunrise on a May morning and they will never be attacked by bugs.

⁓ Set an onion in the center of a hill of cucumbers, squashes, melons, etc., and it will effectually keep off the yellow striped bug that preys upon these plants when young.

—TRADITIONAL

CUCUMBER À LA CRÈME

Peel and cut into slices (lengthwise) some fine cucumbers. Boil them until soft; salt to taste, and serve with delicate cream sauce.

◁FRIED CUCUMBERS▷

Pare them and cut lengthwise in very thick slices; wipe them dry with a cloth; sprinkle with salt and pepper, dredge with flour, and fry in lard and butter, a tablespoon of each, mixed. Brown both sides and serve warm.

—MRS. F. L. GILLETTE, *THE WHITE HOUSE COOK BOOK*

Cucurbitaceous Grou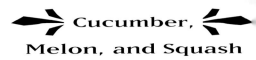

➤ Cucumber, ◄
Melon, and Squash

All members of this group are especially suited to outdoor culture, but they are all very tender to frost. Seeds must be planted somewhat shallow from early spring to midsummer...Fine cucumbers are sometimes grown in hills surrounding a barrel in which manure is placed to be leached out by successive waterings.

—L. H. BAILEY, *GARDEN-MAKING*

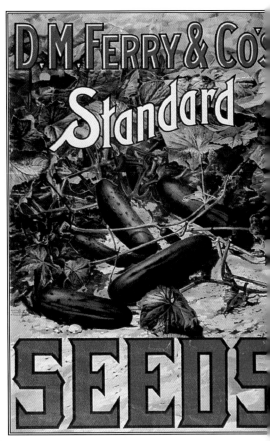

WATERMELON MARMALADE

Weigh twelve pounds rind, previously soaked in brine, and the salt extracted by fresh water; parboil, put on with twelve pounds sugar made into a thin syrup, and boil to pieces. Add the peelings of twelve oranges and twelve lemons, previously soaked in water, cut in strips and boiled extremely soft, the water being changed three times while boiling. Stir constantly from the bottom. Cook very thick. Put in wide-mouth jars.

—MRS. S. T., IN M. C. TYREE, *HOUSEKEEPING IN OLD VIRGINIA*

MELONS
→IN MAY←

"Reckon not your chickens before they are hatched"—that is to say, be not too hasty about the enjoyment of those things which are still far off. Wait patiently until your water-melon is ripe before you eat it. But Stop! we have not yet planted it perhaps—spur up, spur up, boys! the garden must not be neglected.

—*THE OLD FARMER'S ALMANAC*

Tap a watermelon with your fingers, and if the sound is hollow, it is ripe.

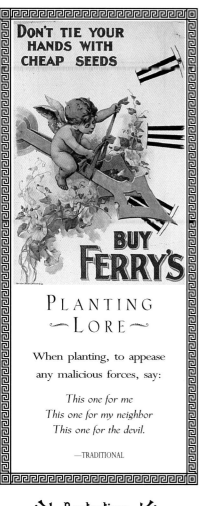

PLANTING ~LORE~

When planting, to appease
any malicious forces, say:

*This one for me
This one for my neighbor
This one for the devil.*

—TRADITIONAL

❊ Nasturtium, ❊ or Indian Cress

The close, compact growth, rich-colored flowers, and the freedom with which nasturtiums bloom, all combine to place them among first-class bedding plants. The seeds when green are often used in pickling, affording an agreeable pungent addition to the contents of the pickle jar.

—*BEETON'S DICTIONARY OF EVERY-DAY GARDENING*

➤ MAY PLANTING ≺

To own a bit of ground, to scratch it with a hoe, to plant seeds and watch their renewal of life,— this is the commonest delight of the race, the most satisfactory thing one can do.

—CHARLES DUDLEY WARNER, *MY SUMMER IN A GARDEN*

RECIPES

CANDIED VIOLETS

Get some fine double blossoms; break off the heads and put into water in which a little isinglass has been dissolved. Put them after this in a little cool spun sugar. Sprinkle the violets with the very finest powdered sugar and lay them to dry in the sun or some warm place, but on no account put them in the oven.

—MRS. CAMERON LUCY,
HEARTS AND SPADES

Chautauqua
Gooseberry

orth Star
urrant

WILDER
EARLY PEAR

Abundance

JUNE

JUNE DAMP AND WARM
DOES THE GARDENER NO HARM.

June

ADVICE

Flower Garden

Lawns will now require to be mowed weekly in all well-kept places. It is as much an indication of slovenliness to see a door-yard that has any pretensions to be called lawn, with the grass uncut, as it would be to see a dust-begrimed carpet in the parlor.

Fruit Garden

If strawberries have not been mulched with hay or straw in winter, the cut grass from the lawn is a convenient thing to place between the rows to keep the fruit from getting sanded by dashing rains. Nearly all small fruits, such as gooseberries, raspberries, etc., etc., are much improved by having a mulching of some sort placed around the roots, which should be done this month.

Vegetable Garden

This is usually the busiest month in the garden; crops mature and have to be gathered and while doing so, weeds are apt to steal a march on you, and may destroy entirely some of your hard work of former months, unless you attack in their embryo stage. Beans, peas, beets, corn, cucumbers, lettuce, etc., may be yet sown for succession crops, and the late plantings of Irish potatoes and sweet potatoes will yet do well on suitable soils. Tomatoes should be tied up to trellises or stakes, if fine-flavored and handsome fruit is desired.

—PETER HENDERSON, *GARDENING FOR PLEASURE*

JUNE

The lily has an air,
And the snowdrop a grace,
And the sweet pea a way,
And the heart's-ease a face—
Yet there's nothing like the rose
When she blows.

—CHRISTINA ROSSETTI, AS QUOTED IN DE GARDENNE BOKE

How to Preserve Green Currants and Gooseberries

In the *Massachusetts Ploughman* a writer says—For the last ten or twelve years I have been in the habit of preserving green currants in considerable quantities for domestic use, and find them not only a luxury, but a great convenience. My mode of preserving them is simply this: I gather the currants or gooseberries while green, put them into dry glass bottles, cork and seal them tight; then place them in the cellar in such a position as is most convenient. In this manner they may be preserved for years.

—JOHN L. BLAKE, D. D., *THE FARMER'S EVERYDAY BOOK*

Currants

Currants delight in a cool, moist soil, and cannot be grown successfully in the southern states. While many growers place them five feet each way, some prefer to have them six or seven feet between the rows. For the first year or two after planting, the currants require but little care in pruning, except to cut back the new shoots about one-half, and if very thick, to remove the weaker ones.

—L. H. BAILEY, *GARDEN-MAKING*

CURRANT ◁ WINE ▷

The currants should be quite ripe. Stem, mash and strain them, adding half a pint of water and less than a pound of sugar to a quart of the mashed fruit. Stir well up together and pour into a clean cask, leaving the bung–hole open, or covered with a piece of lace. It should stand for a month to ferment, when it will be ready for bottling.

—MRS. F. L. GILLETTE, *THE WHITE HOUSE COOK BOOK*

MILDEW ON GOOSEBERRIES

he *Farmer's Gazette* states that the mildew is prevented
by sprinkling fine salt around the bushes; or, where
n be had, by placing seaweed around. Watering with
-suds, before fruit forms, and using compost for
re, is also good.

—JOHN L. BLAKE, D. D., *THE FARMER'S EVERYDAY BOOK*

s easy to propagate currants and gooseberries from
ttings taken from new shoots. Put them in rich
, leaving an inch and one bud above ground, with
or five inches below the surface.

— *THE OLD FARMER'S ALMANAC*

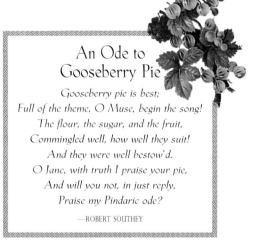

An Ode to Gooseberry Pie

Gooseberry pie is best;
Full of the theme, O Muse, begin the song!
The flour, the sugar, and the fruit,
Commingled well, how well they suit!
And they were well bestow'd.
O Jane, with truth I praise your pie,
And will you not, in just reply,
Praise my Pindaric ode?

—ROBERT SOUTHEY

◁ GOOSEBERRY TARTS ▷

Top and tail gooseberries. Put into a porcelain
kettle with enough water to prevent burning and
stew slowly until they break.
Take them off, sweeten well and
set aside to cool. When cold, pour
into pastry shells and bake with a
top crust of puff paste. Brush all
over with beaten egg while hot;
set back in the oven to glaze for
three minutes. Eat cold.

—MRS. F. L. GILLETTE, *THE WHITE HOUSE COOK BOOK*

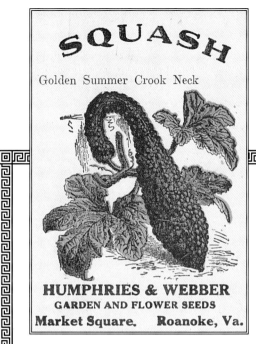

Heresy In Squash Culture

or How to Eat Squash When Other People Are Watching It Blossom

All the garden books tell us to wait until
the danger of frost is past before planting one's squash. We always have our
first squash ready to eat before those
planted in May are in blossom…Compost
makes a famous top dressing and is
spread over the garden in the spring.
Through this source we have been sur-
prised to see how many seeds have the
vitality to survive a winter out of doors.

—GRACE L. WEEKS, *THE GARDEN MAGAZINE*

Squash, tomatoes, and melons must have
their runners cut off, or they, too, will
forget themselves and make a vast
amount more vine than they will of fruit.

—EDITH L. FULLERTON, *HOW TO MAKE A VEGETABLE GARDEN*

Rose growing has come to have much the same aspect as wedlock—a thing not to be entered into lightly, but soberly and most advisedly.

—FRANCES DUNCAN, *LADIES' HOME JOURNAL*

LIBERTY.

PETER HENDERSON & CO., NEW YORK.

ADMIRAL DEWEY.

BALDUIN

WHITE MAMAN COCHET

THE TINCTURE
OF ROSES

Take leaves of the common rose, place them, without pressing them, in a bottle, pour good spirits upon them, close the bottle, and let it stand until it is required for use. The tincture will keep for years, and yield a perfume a little inferior to otto of roses. A few drops of it will suffice to impregnate the atmosphere of a room with a delicious odor. Common vinegar is improved by a very small quantity being added to it.

—JOHN L. BLAKE, D. D.,
THE FARMER'S EVERYDAY BOOK

HENDERSON'S EMPIRE   COLLECTION OF HARDY   EVER BLOOMING ROSES

SALADS

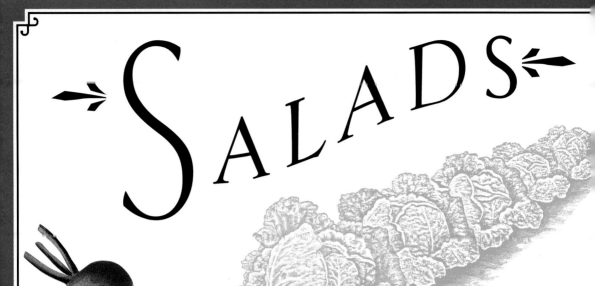

❖ RADISHES ❖

As soon as taken from the ground, put in cold water. Then put red and white radishes alternately in a dish of fanciful design, ornamenting with curled parsley, in the center and around the edges.

—MRS. T., IN M. C. TYREE,
HOUSEKEEPING IN OLD VIRGINIA

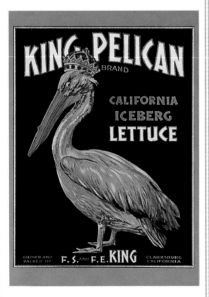

LETTUCE

Food and Fable

The salad which, if we are wise, accompanies most meals is a veritable pot-pourri of old beliefs and legends. Its principal ingredient, lettuce—which, as we sometimes forget, means milky vegetable, from its sap—was not only the favorite food of beautiful Adonis, but shared with Juno the parentage of pretty Hebe, to whom the Queen of Heaven gave birth as a consequence of eating the crisp plant.

—WALTER RICHARDS,
THE LIVING AGE

Lettuce is like conversation: it must be fresh and crisp, so sparkling that you can scarcely notice the bitter in it. Lettuce, like most talkers, is, however, apt to run rapidly to seed...Lettuce, like conversation, requires a good deal of oil, to avoid friction, and keep the company smooth.

—CHARLES DUDLEY WARNER,
MY SUMMER IN A GARDEN

LETTUCE DRESSED

Take well-headed lettuce, chop it fine and pour over a dressing made of salt and pepper, mustard, hard-boiled egg, and olive oil. Cream the yolk of the egg and mustard together with a little oil, until quite smooth. Add vinegar if desired.

—MRS. R., IN M. C. TYREE,
HOUSEKEEPING IN OLD VIRGINIA

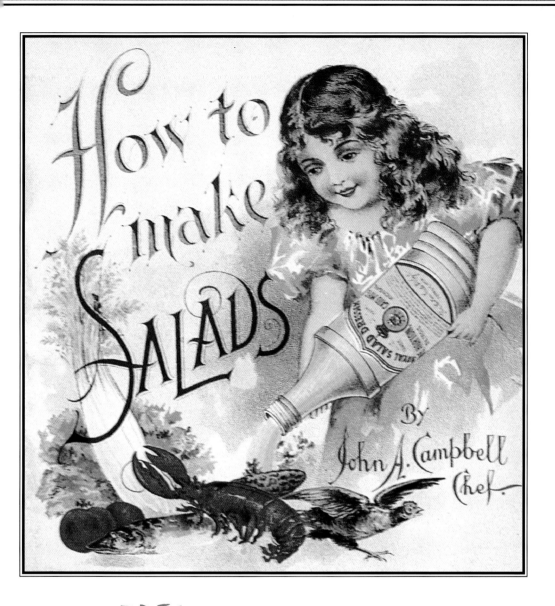

How to make SALADS

By John A. Campbell, Chef

If possible, use vegetables gathered in the early morning, with the dew on them. It is even better to gather late the evening before, with the evening dew on them (setting them in the ice-house, or some cool place), than to gather them after the morning sun has grown hot. If you are living in the city, get your vegetables from market as early in the morning as possible.

—M. C. TYREE, *HOUSEKEEPING IN OLD VIRGINIA*

If leaves come to you sadly wilted, place them in a pan of cold water, for they are nothing more or less than a handful of plants asking for a drink.

—EDITH L. FULLERTON, *HOW TO MAKE A VEGETABLE GARDEN*

RICE'S POPULAR
FLOWER SEEDS

JULY

CUT A THISTLE IN JUNE, HE'LL COME AGAIN SOON,
CUT HIM IN JULY, AND HE'S SURE TO DIE.

Jerome B.
CAMBR

July

ADVICE

Flower Garden

Plants such as dahlias, roses, gladioli, as well as many herbaceous perennial and annual plants, will now require staking; be careful to proportion the size of the stake to that of the plant, and do not tie it too tightly. Carnations and other plants that are throwing up flower stems, if wanted to flower in winter, should be cut back.

Fruit Garden

The fruit will now be gathered from the strawberry vines, and if new beds are to be formed, the system recommended of layering the plants in small pots is the best. Where apples, pears, peaches, etc., have set fruit thickly, thin out one-half or two-thirds of the young fruit, as by doing so you will get at least an equal weight and much finer fruit.

Vegetable Garden

Plants of cabbages, cauliflowers, celery, and all similar varieties of vegetables wanted for fall or winter use are best planted this month though in some sections they will do if left until next...Sweet corn, beans, cucumbers and lettuce may yet be planted for late crops, and in some sections rutabaga turnips for the main winter crop. Tomatoes should be kept tied up to stakes or trellises, and sweet potatoes must be hoed so as to prevent the vines rooting at the joints.

—PETER HENDERSON,
GARDENING FOR PLEASURE

JULY

It has long been known that the juice of a wild pansy dropped into the eye of a sleeping person will cause them to fall in love with the first person they see.

—TRADITIONAL

PETER HENDERSON & CO'S COLLECTION
OF
10 FLORAL BEAUTIES

GAILLARDIA—NEW HYBRIDS, MIXED.
Per Packet, 15 cents.

PANSY—BRILLIANT.
Per Packet, 25 cents.

NASTURTIUMS—New Tom Thumb, Mixed.
Per Packet, 10 cents.

POPPY—FIRE DRAGON.
Per Packet, 25 cents.

VERBENA—HENDERSON'S MAMMOTH.
Per Packet, 25 cents.

GODETIA—NAMELESS BEAUTY.
Per Packet, 25 cents.

DIANTHUS—Large Flowering, Fringed.
Per Packet, 10 cents.

SWEET PEAS—Eckford's Newest Hybrids.
Per Packet, 15 cents.

GIVING A GRAND
→ DISPLAY ←
During the entire
SEASON.

ASTER—TRIUMPH.
Per Packet, 25 cents.

PHLOX—STAR OF QUEDLINBURG.
Per Packet, 25 cents.

FULL COLLECTION
ONE PACKET OF EACH
OF 10 FLORAL BEAUTIES
FREE BY MAIL FOR
$1.25
THEIR COST SEPARATELY IS 2.00

Fitting the House to the Flower Garden

I once knew a worthy lady who painted her house to harmonize with some magnificent rhododendrons which grew near it, and every passer-by who admired the rhododendrons blessed her unaware. Yet only around the corner, beside a house of reddish brown, was an unhappy azalea—aflame in that crimson-magenta which, as far as quarrelsomeness is concerned, carries a chip on its shoulder—and not even an evergreen in between to break the violence of color. Far from enjoying the blooming of the unfortunate plant, one could only be thankful when it was over.

—FRANCES DUNCAN, *LADIES' HOME JOURNAL*

Summer Flowers

The chief use of flowers is to
illustrate quotations from the poets.

—DE GARDENNE BOKE

Floral Arranging

The flowers are of all heights (the stems of different lengths), and, though massed, are in broken and irregular ranks, the tallest standing a little over two [fee]t high. But there is no crushing or crowding. Each [ind]ividual has room to display its full perfection. The [col]or gathers, softly flushing from the snow white at one [en]d, through all the rose, pink, cherry and crimson [sha]des, to the note of darkest red; the long stems of ten-[de]r green showing through the clear glass, the radiant [ta]pered gold of each flower illuminating the whole.

—CELIA THAXTER, AN ISLAND GARDEN

TO PRESERVE ❖ BOUQUETS ❖

Put a little saltpeter in the water you use for your bouquets and the flowers will live for a fortnight.

—MRS. F. L. GILLETTE, THE WHITE HOUSE COOK BOOK

To me the meanest flower that blows can give
Thoughts that do often lie too deep for tears.
—WILLIAM WORDSWORTH, AS QUOTED IN DE GARDENNE BOKE

Flowers will bloom over and over again in poems, as in the summer fields, to the end of time, always old and always new. Why should we be more shy of repeating ourselves than the Spring be tired of blossoms or the night of stars?

—OLIVER WENDELL HOLMES, AS QUOTED IN DE GARDENNE BOKE

Morning—glory at my window satisfies me more
than the metaphysics of books.
—WALT WHITMAN

If a garden contains crocuses, tulips, peonies, irises and rudbeckias, these, in their order, will bloom from crocus time in May to rudbeckia days in the early fall. As a matter of fact nearly all the flowers bloom by the end of July, but with careful management the garden may be filled with flowers the summer long.

—ZONA GALE, THE OUTING MAGAZINE

❖ STRAWBERRIES ❖

The low-growing, virtually evergreen strawberries with their beautifully formed leaves are in some respects very human. Their children (the runners) are always moving away and making new homes for themselves; also relying on the good mother plant for guidance and support, which she supplies through the leading string.

—EDITH L. FULLERTON, *HOW TO MAKE A VEGETABLE GARDEN*

The neighbor's small children are out of place in your garden, in strawberry and currant time. I hope I appreciate the value of children…But the problem is, what to do with them in a garden. For they are not good to eat, and there is a law against making away with them…I, for one, feel that it would not be right, aside from the law, to take the life, even of the smallest child, for the sake of a little fruit, more or less, in the garden.

—CHARLES DUDLEY WARNER, *MY SUMMER IN A GARDEN*

STRAWBERRY PRESERVE

Cap the berries. Put one and a half pounds sugar to ... pound fruit. Let them stand two or three hours, and ... boil thirty minutes.

—MRS. R., IN M. C. TYREE, *HOUSEKEEPING IN OLD VIRGINIA*

STRAWBERRY JELLY

Pick the strawberries, put them into a pan, squeeze t... well with a wooden spoon, add sufficient pounded suga... sweeten them nicely, and let them remain for one hour ... the juice may be extracted; then add a half pint of wate... every pint of juice. Strain the strawberry juice and w... through a napkin; measure it and for every pint allow ... a package of Cox's gelatin dissolved in a tea cupfu... water. Mix this with the juice, and put the jelly into a m... and set the mold on ice.

—MRS. F. L. GILLETTE, *THE WHITE HOUSE COOK BOOK*

Food and Fable

The strawberry has both a pagan and a Christian reputation. It was a favorite of the goddess Frigga, who was wont to go a-berrying with the children at the summer solstice. Afterwards it was placed under the patronage of the Blessed Virgin, and on St. John's Day, "no mother who has lost a little child will taste a strawberry, for if she did, her little one would get none in Paradise."

—WALTER RICHARDS, *THE LIVING AGE*

Never eat the first strawberry—throw it where the birds will get it.

HERBS and MEDICINAL PLANTS

HYSSOP

BALM.

→ The Herb Garden ←

The *olitory,* or herb-garden, is a department of horticulture somewhat neglected, and yet the culture and curing of simples was formerly a part of a lady's education. All the sweet herbs are pretty, and a strip of ground half-way between the kitchen and the flower-garden would keep them more immediately under the eye of the mistress. This would probably recover, for our soups and salads, some of the neglected tarragons, French sorrel, purslain, chervil, dill, and clary, which are now only found in the pages of old herbals.

—BEETON'S NEW DICTIONARY OF EVERY-DAY GARDENING

MEDICINAL PROPERTIES OF THE GARDEN'S BOUNTY

...ach has a direct effect upon the ...plaints of the kidneys; asparagus ...ies the blood; celery acts ...rably upon the nervous system, ...is a cure for rheumatism and ...algia; tomatoes act upon the ...; beets and turnips are excellent ...tizers; lettuce and cucumbers ...cooling in their effects upon the ...m; beans are a very nutritious ...strengthening vegetable; white ...ns, garlic, leeks, chives and shal- ...all of which are similar, possess ...cinal virtues of a marked char- ..., stimulating the circulatory ...m, and the consequent increase ...e saliva and the gastric juice ...noting digestion.

—MRS. F. L. GILLETTE,
THE WHITE HOUSE COOK BOOK

...ACK-CURRANT TEA

...two tablespoons of black- ...ant jam in a jug and pour a pint ...oiling water into it. A cooling ...k and excellent for a cold, ...cially in the throat.

—MRS. CAMERON LUCY, *HEARTS AND SPADES*

PARSLEY
MOSS CURLED

HERB LORE

⁓ Parsley flourishes where the Missus is master.

⁓ Objects containing caraway seed cannot be stolen, including a husband with a few in his pocket.

⁓ Early Americans called dill seeds "Meeting House Seeds" because they chewed them to relieve their boredom during long sermons.

⁓ Sprinkle parsley seed on the head three times a year to reverse the effects of balding.

⁓ Marjoram mixed with honey and applied to the skin will remove bruises.

—TRADITIONAL

SAGE

MOCK PARSLEY

When parsley is not to be had, tie up a little parsley seed in a piece of muslin and lay this in the sauce, gravy, etc., you wish to flavor, adding where the green leaves are necessary come finely minced and blanched spinach or other green stuff.

—MRS. CAMERON LUCY, *HEARTS AND SPADES*

SWEET BASIL

THIEVES' VINEGAR

A handful of sage and the same of mint, tansy, rue, rosemary, lavender, and thyme; one ounce of camphor. Put in a gallon demijohn, and fill with good vinegar. Set in the sun for two weeks with a piece over the mouth, then stop tightly.

—MRS. D. R., IN M. C. TYREE,
HOUSEKEEPING IN OLD VIRGINIA

AUGUST

IF THE TWENTY-FOURTH OF AUGUST BE FAIR AND CLEAR,
THEN HOPE FOR A PROSPEROUS AUTUMN THAT YEAR.

August
ADVICE

Flower Garden

The Instructions for July apply with but little variation in this department this month.

ZINNIAS

Fruit Garden

All [strawberry] runners should be kept cut off close to the old plant. If plants are wanted for fresh plantations, about the required number can be allowed to run, but should be layered in pots. Cut away the old stems of raspberries and blackberries that have borne their fruit, and thin out the young shoots to three or four canes to each hill or plant, if tied to stakes and topped when four or five feet high, they will make stronger canes for fruiting next year.

Vegetable Garden

Planted crops, such as cabbage, cauliflower, and celery, should be hoed deeply. We do not recommend the earthing up of celery this month. Onions will in many sections now be ready for harvesting; this condition will be

PARSNIP

known by the tops becoming yellow and falling down; they are best dried by placing them in some dry shed in thin layers. Spinach may be sown for early fall use, but it is yet too early to sow for the winter crop. Red-top, White Globe, and Yellow Aberdeen turnips should now be sown. Rutabaga turnips sown last month will need thinning.

—PETER HENDERSON, *GARDENING FOR PLEASURE*

AUGUST

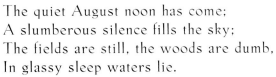

The quiet August noon has come;
A slumberous silence fills the sky;
The fields are still, the woods are dumb,
In glassy sleep waters lie.

—W. C. BRYANT, *THE OLD FARMER'S ALMANAC*

HOT PEPPERS

Quaint, little, fierce-tempered, red headed creatures—but we love them for all that! Full well does the housewife who takes pride in her pickles and preserves realize how essential they are. Peppers are easily grown. Take good care of the seedlings, and when past their infancy they are but little trouble.

—EDITH L. FULLERTON, *COUNTRY LIFE IN AMERICA*

❖ Peppers planted by an angry ❖ gardener or a lunatic will be hotter.

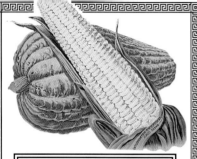

CORN

"My corn grew so high it was shading my tomatoes too much, so I just cut off the top of the bloomin' things."

"Had it tasseled?" we inquired.

"It was just beginning. Why?"

We answered him with another question. "Is there any corn planted near yours?"

"No, not very near. Why?"

An alarmed expression came over his face when we told him that the powder on the tassel fell on the silk fringe hanging from the ear, and that this powder made the corn develop and grow, otherwise there would be no crop. He was perfectly dumbfounded.

—EDITH L. FULLERTON,
HOW TO MAKE A VEGETABLE GARDEN

Salzer's New Golden Combination Corn.

Surely old mother earth outdid herself in producing this new golden yellow dent corn prodigy. Golden wonder of all corns! Thou art early and vigorous, new blooded, and in quality perfect; yea, a colossal, p yielder. This marvelous corn is more fully described on the inside cover of this catalogue.

Price, big package, will give you seed for 10 acres in 1902, 15c.; pint, 20c.; quart, 50c.; postpaid. By freight half bushel, $1.50; bushel, $3.50; two and one-half bushels, $5.00. Five bushels or more at $1.75 a bushel.

The Best Way to Water Your Garden

If the plants are in rows one of the best ways of watering is to make a deep furrow with the hoe, fill this with water, let it soak in; fill again and yet once more, then replace the soil, and every drop of water has gone where the plants most need it, and the excellent habit the roots have formed of extending down for water is not corrupted.

—FRANCES DUNCAN,
LADIES' HOME JOURNAL

DROUGHT and What to Do About It

Probably the greatest anxiety of the gardener will be about the water supply. The delicately-clad maiden, who, watering pot in hand, walks in the garden in the cool of the day and sprinkles lightly the plants, is a pleasing vision and one which has always been dear to the poets, but a gardener has scant use for her. The watering at evening is well enough, and the sprinkling always pleasant to the leaves, but daily sprinkling as a means of giving the roots a drink is an invention of the Serpent and one of the things he would surely have taught Eve when he set about spoiling her gardening in Paradise.

—FRANCES DUNCAN, *LADIES' HOME JOURNAL*

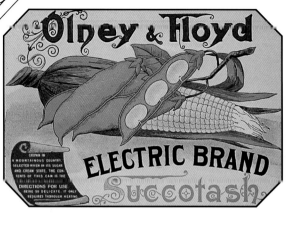

A little corn left over today, with a few beans, makes succotash for tomorrow.

—MRS. S. T. RORER, *LADIES' HOME JOURNAL*

Hints to the Cook

⚬ It is said that a good vegetable cook never needs a garbage bucket.

—MRS. S. T. RORER, *LADIES' HOME JOURNAL*

⚬ The easiest way to have home-grown vegetables in November and December is to make a coldframe, and during the last week of August transplant into it young lettuce and spinach from the garden.

⚬ The early crop of celery will soon be nearly full grown. Then begin to blanch it.

⚬ Have you any surplus of early apples? Are you canning any peaches?

—THE GARDEN MAGAZINE

⚬ Do not throw beets and turnips and potatoes all into the same box; have small boxes and keep each vegetable separate.

⚬ Peaches are best gathered early in the day or late. They bruise more if gathered whilst the sun is on them.

—MRS. CAMERON LUCY,
HEARTS AND SPADES

 # THREE RECIPES

FROM VIRGINIA HOUSEWIVES

LIMA BEANS

Shell and lay in cold water. Put in boiling water an hour before dinner; add some salt; when tender, drain off the water and add a tablespoon fresh butter. Beans are seldom cooked enough. —MRS. S. T.

BAKED TOMATOES

Scald and peel the tomatoes, or else peel thin with a sharp knife, without scalding. Cut in small pieces, and season with a little sugar, salt, pepper, and finely minced onion. Grease a baking dish and line it with thin slices of light bread, buttered. Pour the tomatoes in the dish, crumbling up a little light bread on them. Spread on top a layer of heavily buttered light bread, and bake. —MRS. M. C. C.

TO DRESS CUCUMBERS RAW

Gather early in the morning, peel, lay in cold water til just before dinner. Then drain, slice as thin as possible into ice water, which drain and then fill a dish with alternate layers of sliced cucumber and thinly sliced white onion, sprinkled with salt and pepper. Pour a cup of weak vinegar over it and lay a lump of ice on top. —MRS. S. T.

 —M. C. TYREE, *HOUSEKEEPING IN OLD VIRGINIA*

RECIPES

Almost all vegetables are better if they are prepared for cooking early in the morning and soaked in cold water until cooking time...All vegetables should go over a fire in boiling water, [with salt added] to the green vegetables.

—MRS. S. T. RORER, *LADIES' HOME JOURNAL*

SEPTEMBER

SEPTEMBER BLOWS SOFT
TILL THE FRUIT'S IN THE LOFT.

September
ADVICE

Flower Garden

Holland bulbs, such as hyacinths, tulips, etc., etc., and most varieties of lilies may be planted this month. Violets that are wanted for winter will now be growing freely, and the runners should be trimmed off as recommended for strawberries last month.

Fruit Garden

New plantations of strawberry plants may now be made from the runners that have been layered in pots; the sooner in the month they are planted, the stronger they will be for next season. Attend to raspberries and blackberries as advised last month, if not then done.

OH! HOW STRONG I AM.

GROWN & PUT UP BY

JEROME B. RICE & CO.

CAMBRIDGE VALLEY CAMBRIDGE, N.Y.
SEED GARDENS,

RICE'S SEEDS

Vegetable Garden

Seeds of cabbage, cauliflower, and lettuce to raise plants to be placed in cold frames, should be sown…the main crop of spinach or sprouts that is wanted for winter or spring use, should be sown about same dates. Celery may now have the earth drawn to it with the hoe preparatory to earthing-up by the spade. Onions that were not dried and harvested last month, must be done this, or it will be too late. The early or flat sorts of turnips may yet be sown the first week of this month.

—PETER HENDERSON, *GARDENING FOR PLEASURE*

SEPTEMBER

It was autumn that I met
Her whom I love; the sunflowers bold
Stood up like guards around her set,
And all the air with mignonette
Was warm within the garden old.

—DORA GREENWELL

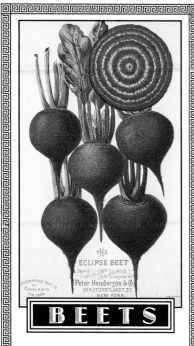

THE ECLIPSE BEET

Drawn, Engraved and Printed from Nature by

Peter Henderson & Co.
35 & 37 CORTLANDT ST.
NEW YORK.

DESCRIPTION PAGE 2 OF CATALOGUE FOR 1898

BEETS

"What is this?" I cried at once.

"Beet-greens," said my wife.

"They can't be, I returned. "They're not the least bit stringy."

"But they are beet-greens," my wife assured me. "Our neighbor sent them."

Then and there I learned the difference between vegetables which go directly from the garden to the pot and those which have spent two days in becoming dry and tough. I also tasted, for the first time, the little tender beets which are the proper accompaniment and the crowning relish to greens from the home-garden. And if beets were so, what of peas and beans, spinach, and corn, and tomatoes, and all the rest? The revelation from that one mouthful was surprising.

—ALLEN FRENCH,
COUNTRY LIFE IN AMERICA

Cabbage Recipes

⊲ COLD SLAW ⊳

Wash your cabbage and lay in cold water some hours. Have a seasoning of egg, mustard, oil, pepper, salt, celery-seed, and vinegar, and pour over it. In winter the slaw will keep a day or two.

MRS. W., IN M. C. TYREE, *HOUSEKEEPING IN OLD VIRGINIA*

Of all the vegetables in common use I look upon the cabbage as my best friend. When well-headed and bleached it is more dainty than any member of its family, not excepting Brussels sprouts nor savoy. In the hands of a dainty and artistic cook, it lends itself to a great variety of dishes and is superior in flavor and color than its more aristocratic relative, the cauliflower.

—MRS. S. T. RORER, *LADIES' HOME JOURNAL*

✤ PICKLING ✤

or pickles and catsups, use the best cider vinegar,
it being not only more wholesome than other
s of vinegar, but the only sort that will keep
les or catsup for any length of time.

reparing pickles: Vegetables for pickle should be
kept in cold water and strong brine till they turn
ow; then put vine-leaves in the bottom of the
le, then a layer of vegetables and a layer of leaves
ull. Pour on them boiling salt and water and let
n boil until a bright green. Take them, while hot,
place in weak vinegar for a whole week.

n add to them the spiced vinegar. Afterwards rub
them a little turmeric. Prepare the spiced vinegar
May, and expose to the sun everyday for some
. —MRS. R.

◁ PICKLE VINEGAR ▷

2 GALLONS VINEGAR.	2 POUNDS SUGAR.
I OUNCE TURMERIC.	3 OUNCES ALLSPICE.
I OUNCE CLOVES.	I OUNCE MACE.
I PINT MUSTARD-SEED.	2 TABLESPOONS CELERY-SEED.

Pound together and stir into the hot cider vinegar for
several minutes. Prepare your vegetables by quartering
the cabbage and scalding them in brine; cover them and
leave until cold; squeeze dry and hang in the sun; when
bleached, throw in plain vinegar, then into the spiced
vinegar. —MRS. P.

—M. C. TYREE, *HOUSEKEEPING IN OLD VIRGINIA*

ONIONS
PRIZETAKER

Price
10
Cents

BURT'S SEED FOR QUALITY

How to Preserve
❖ TOMATOES ❖

Take clean, ripe tomatoes, sufficient to cover the bott
of a large kettle, and place it over a slow fire until t
skins break, which must be then peeled off; cut out
hard core, and slowly boil the remainder until it becom
quite thick, and of a dark-brown color, stirring it well
prevent burning. Spread it upon plates about an inch in
thickness, and dry in the sun for seven days, afterwards
placing it in a moderately warm oven until thoroughly
dried. The substance thus prepared will keep for years,
and is so highly flavored, that a piece two-inches squar
stewed in a half a teacupful of water, will be sufficient t
mix with the gravy of five pounds of beefsteak.

—JOHN L. BLAKE, D. D., *THE FARMER'S EVERYDAY BOOK*

TO BAKE ONIONS

Boil six onions in water, or milk and water with seasoning of pepper and salt. When done enough to mash, take
them off, mash them with butter, grate bread crumbs
over them and set them to bake. Or place them whole in
the baking dish with butter and bread crumbs.

TO COOK ONIONS

Boil until tender, in milk and water. Pour melted butter
over them, and serve; or chop up and stew with a little
milk, butter and salt.

—MRS. S. T., IN M. C. TYREE, *HOUSEKEEPING IN OLD VIRGINIA*

TOMATO
SOUP

Squeeze out tw
tomatoes into
cupful of mil
Let it boil, the
add a little whi
sauce and crea
sauce to taste.

—MRS. CAMERON LUCY
HEARTS AND SPADES

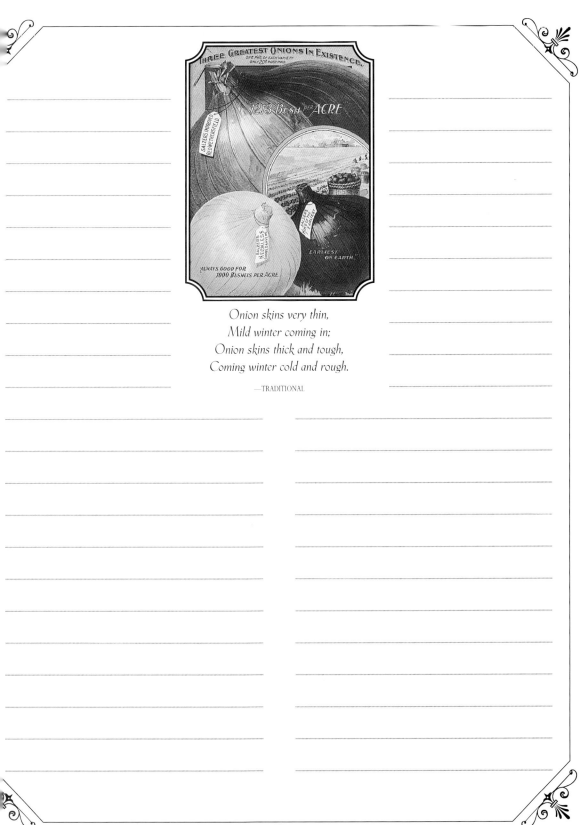

Onion skins very thin,
Mild winter coming in;
Onion skins thick and tough,
Coming winter cold and rough.

—TRADITIONAL

CANNING

Saving the Garden's Surplus

If this is your first flight in the art of preserving, study all the devices to make labor as light as possible and have the result as great a success as may be. Don't for one moment contemplate tins; they are villains in disguise, besides being usable but once and then a burden to the household to dispose of. Glass is good forever.

Vegetables should be parboiled in salted water before being placed in the jars: this removes any acrid quality, without destroying the flavor.

Different vegetables need different times for the parboiling because of their varying textures, depending also to some degree on the age and tenderness. The average times are:

PEAS	8 MINUTES
STRING BEANS	4 MINUTES
CAULIFLOWER	4 MINUTES
LIMA BEANS	15 MINUTES
CARROTS	15 MINUTES
TURNIPS	15 MINUTES
SPINACH	6 MINUTES

"What to Can" Is as Important as "How to Ca[n]"

Fruits for canning should be selec[ted] as much with a view to the ultim[ate] color as for flavor. There are red-fleshed and white-fleshed strawbe[r]ries; take the former. And in plu[ms] what more pleasing than the rich red of the Satsuma plum—superb when canned but useless to eat o[ut] of the hand!

To Prevent Cracking of Bottles and Fruit Jars

If a bottle or fruit jar that has been more than once used is placed on a towel thoroughly soaked in hot water, there is little danger of its being cracked by the introduction of hot liquid.

Tips for Making
Preserves and Fruit Jellies

The best peaches for preserving, brandying, or pickling, are white freestone peaches, not quite ripe enough to eat with cream. Pears and quinces also should be preserved before they are quite ripe enough for eating. They should be parboiled before eating. No fruit should be over-ripe when preserved. Damsons and blue plums should be slit lengthwise with a pen knife, and set in the sun before preserving, which will render it easy to extract the stones. Cherries also should be stoned before preserving.

Always make preserves in a porcelain or brass kettle. If the latter, have it scoured first with sand, then with salt and vinegar. Then scald it and put in the sugar and water for the syrup.

In peeling fruit, throw it into cold water to keep it from turning dark, and let it remain there till you are ready to throw it in the boiling syrup. Bear in mind that exposure to the air turns peeled fruit dark.

Cut sugar is best for preserves which you wish to be clear and light-colored, but nice brown sugar is best for dark-colored jams and marmalades, such as those made of blackberries, raspberries, whortleberries, etc.

—M. C. TYREE, *HOUSEKEEPING IN OLD VIRGINIA*

PETER HENDERSON & CO.

35 & 37 CORTLAND
NEW YORK

EMPEROR
NARCISSUS see page 16

CATALOGUE OF

BULBS

PLANTS
AND SEEDS

FOR
Autumn
Planting

OCTOBER

DRY YOUR BARLEY-LAND IN OCTOBER
OR YOU'LL ALWAYS BE SOBER.

October
ADVICE

Flower Garden

The planting of fall bulbs of all kinds may continue during this month. Dahlias, tuberoses, gladiolus, cannas, caladiums, and all other tender bulbs or tubers that are planted in spring should be taken up before the end of the month, dried and stowed away in some place free of frost during winter.

Fruit Garden

Strawberries that have been layered in pots may yet be planted this month; great care should be taken to trim off runners from early plantings. All kinds of fruit trees and shrubs may be set out; if planting is deferred to the last of the month, the ground around the roots should be mulched to the thickness of three to four inches, with leaves, straw, or rough manure, as a protection to the roots against frost.

Vegetable Garden

This is one of the busiest fall months in the kitchen garden; celery will now be in full growth, and will require close attention to earthing-up, and during the last part of the month, the first lot may be stored away in trenches for the winter…Rhubarb and asparagus, if wanted for use in winter, should be taken up in large clumps and stowed away…and will be fit for use from January to March, according to the temperature of the house.

—PETER HENDERSON, *GARDENING FOR PLEASURE*

OCTOBER

If a maiden wants to know who she will marry, she must walk backwards into a garden on Halloween and place a knife in the leek patch and she will have a vision of her future husband.

—TRADITIONAL

POTATOES

Every attentive observer has noticed that potatoes are of the best quality after they have come to maturity and while they are yet in the ground. The longer they are dug and exposed to light and air, the more this fine flavor is gone, till it is wholly lost and they become unpalatable and unwholesome. Potatoes that remain all winter in the earth where they grew, are in excellent condition for the table in the spring.

—THE OLD FARMER'S ALMANAC

✦ POTATO SNOW ✦

Peel and boil in a saucepan, six large mealy white potatoes. Add a little salt to the water. Take them out one by one, leaving the saucepan in the fire. Rub through a sieve into a deep dish, letting it fall in a mound. Do not touch with a spoon or the hand. Have a sauce-boat of melted butter to serve it with at the table.

—MRS. S. T., IN M. C. TYREE, HOUSEKEEPING IN OLD VIRGINIA

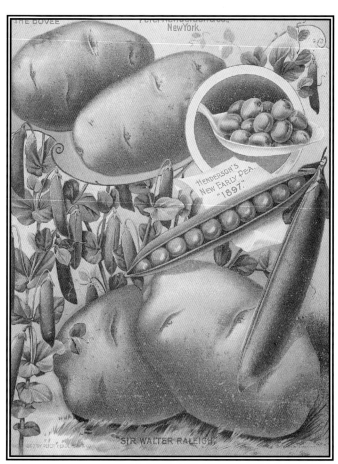

The Golden Pumpkin

Last spring I found a pumpkin seed,
And thought that I would go
And plant it in a secret place,
That no one else would know,
And watch all summer long to see
It grow, and grow, and grow,
And maybe raise a pumpkin for
A Jack-a-lantern show.
I stuck a stick beside the seed,
And I thought that I should shout
One morning when I stooped and saw
The greenest little sprout!
I used to carry water there,
When no one was about,
And every day I'd count to see
How many leaves were out.
Till by and by there came a flower
The color of the sun,
Which withered up, and then I saw
The pumpkin was begun,
But oh! I knew I'd have to wait
So long to have my fun,
Before that green ball could be
A great yellow one.

—MRS. ARCHIBALD, JOURNEYS THROUGH BOOKLAND

As American as Apples

is conceded in Europe that, for size, sound-
ness, flavor, and brilliancy of coloring, the
American apple stands first—a long way
…First, as to the tree. It is so easy of propa-
on, that any man who is capable of learning
to raise a crop of corn can learn how to plant,
t or bud, transplant, and prune an apple tree—
then to eat the apples. It is a thoroughly
thy and hardy tree; and that under more con-
ons and under greater varieties of stress than
haps any other tree…If there is a lot too steep
the plow or too rocky for tools, the farmer
icates it to the apple orchard. Nor do the trees
ay his trust. Yet, the apple loves the meadows.
vill thrive in sandy loams, and adapt itself to
ghest clay. It will bear as a mullein stalk, and as
h wet, almost, as a willow. In short it is a gen-
Democrat…

—HENRY WARD BEECHER,
PLEASANT TALK ABOUT FRUITS, FLOWERS AND FARMING

Burn's Sämling.

nual Catalogue 1905

"Minnetonka,"
Minnesota's Great
Seedling Apple

BOILED CIDER

Boiled cider, in our grandmothers' time, was indis-
pensable to the making of a good "mince pie," adding
the proper flavor and richness, which cannot be sub-
stituted by any other ingredient…Place five quarts of
sweet cider in a porcelain-lined kettle over the fire,
boil it slowly until reduced to one quart, carefully
watching it so that it does not burn; turn into glass
jars while hot and seal tightly.

—MRS. F. L. GILLETTE, *THE WHITE HOUSE COOK BOOK*

APPLE SAUCE

Pare and slice some tart apples; stew until tender in a
very little water, then reduce to a smooth pulp. Stir in
sugar and butter to the taste, a squeeze of lemon juice,
and a little nutmeg.

—MRS. S. T., IN M. C. TYREE, *HOUSEKEEPING IN OLD VIRGINIA*

An aged man, when occupied in grafting an apple-tree, was interrupted by the interrogation, "Why do this, when you cannot expect to live and eat the fruit?" He replied, "Some one planted trees before I was born, and I have eaten the fruit; I now do the same for others, that my gratitude may be known when I am dead."

—JOHN L. BLAKE, D. D.,
THE FARMER'S EVERYDAY BOOK

The Virtues of Compost

at should be done with the remnants of summer's
nty? Do not waste them, anyway. Bean and pea
s should always go into the compost heap and so
ld beet tops, carrot tops, melon vines, etc. Corn
ld be burned, as it seems too large and coarse for
compost heap, and asparagus must be cut partly
burned.

—EDITH L. FULLERTON, *HOW TO MAKE A VEGETABLE GARDEN*

npost piles are the very life of gardening…You
in to make them in the fall, and add to
m through the spring and
mer. Last year's pile is
ly for distribution
in October or the
t of November—that is,
before winter sets in.
will find that you have
lost over five percent of
nitrogen in the course
decomposition, whereas
n manure as generally
ributed, loses from
y to seventy-
percent.

ture works all
mmer weaving at
lions of looms, to
de us and the earth,
l when the work is
ne she shakes off the
ves to keep the earth
rm during the zero
ather. It is a won-
-ful gift and that
n is a fool who
ects it.

—EBEN E. REXFORD,
THE OUTING MAGAZINE

OCTOBER
~LORE~

Half this month you are clearing up
after the past season. And the other half
preparing for the new one. In fine
weather ply the hoe freely between
standing crops. Securely tie up plants
from October gales. On cold nights
cover tender plants with newspapers
pegged down with stones.

—MRS. CAMERON LUCY, *HEARTS AND SPADES*

If the October moon comes without
frost, expect no frost till the full moon
of November. Never burn the peelings of corn, potatoes, bean pods, etc.,
or the hot sun will similarly scorch the
next season's crop. Rolling thunder
in the fall foretells a hard winter. It
is considered important for each member
of the family to taste the new potato
crop, or it may rot. If apples fall off
the tree at the slightest touch, they are
too ripe to keep well.

—TRADITIONAL

ETIQUETTE

➤ DINNER GIVING ←

There are certain established laws by which "dinner giving" is regulated by polite society; and it may not be amiss to give a few observances in relation to them.

A few choice flowers make a charming variety in the appearance of even the most simply laid table, and a pleasing variety at table is quite as essential to the enjoyment of the repast as is a good choice of dishes, for the eye, in fact, should be gratified as much as the palate.

All dishes should be arranged in harmony with the decorations of the flowers, such as covers, relishes, confectionery, and small sweets.

—MRS. F. L. GILLETTE, *THE WHITE HOUSE COOK BOOK*

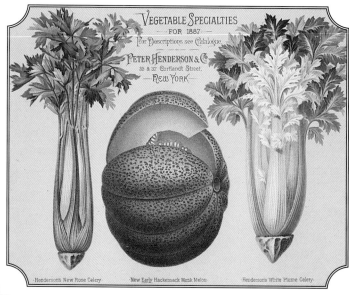

VEGETABLE SPECIALTIES
FOR 1887
For Descriptions see Catalogue.

PETER HENDERSON & CO.
35 & 37 Cortlandt Street.
—NEW YORK—

·Henderson's New Rose Celery·   ·New Early Hackensack Musk Melon·   ·Henderson's White Plume Celery·

➤ Small Points on Table Etiquette

↪ Delicacy of manner at table stamps both man and woman, for one can, a glance, discern whether a person been trained to eat well—i.e., to h the knife and fork properly, to eat without the slightest sound of the li to drink quietly, to use the napkin rightly, to make no noise with any the implements of the table, and las but not least, to eat slowly and masticate the food thoroughly.

↪ Don't, when you drink, elevate you glass as if you were going to stand inverted on your nose. Bring the gla perpendicularly to the lips, and lift i at a slight angle. Do this easily.

↪ Ladies have frequently an affected w of holding the knife half-way down length, as if it were too big for thei little hands; but this is as awkward a way as it is weak; the knife should grasped freely by the handle only.

↪ At the conclusion of a course where they have been used, knife and fork should be laid side by side across the middle of the plate—never crossed; the old custom of crossing them was in obedience to an ancien religious formula.

↪ A spoon should never be turned in the mouth.

—MRS. F. L. GILLETTE, *THE WHITE HOUSE COOK BOOK*

THE FINE ART OF DINING

Let us mention a few things concerning the eating of which there is sometimes doubt. Asparagus—which should be always served on bread or toast so as to absorb super-fluous moisture—may be taken from the finger or the thumb; if it is fit to be set before you, the whole of it may be eaten. Peas and beans, as we all know, require the fork only; however, food that cannot be held with a fork should be eaten with a spoon. Potatoes, if mashed, should be mashed with the fork. Celery, cresses, olives, radishes, and relishes of that kind are, of course, to be eaten with the fingers; the salt should be laid upon one's plate, not upon the cloth. Green corn should be eaten from the cob; but it must be held with a single hand. Fresh fruit should be eaten with a silver-bladed knife, especially pears, apples, etc. Berries, of course, are to be eaten with a spoon.

⇒ PEAS. ⇐

—MRS. F. L. GILLETTE, *THE WHITE HOUSE COOK BOOK*

JOSEPH BRECK & SONS

ESTABLISHED 1822.

NOVEMBER

IF ON THE TREES THE LEAVES STILL HOLD,
THE COMING WINTER WILL BE COLD.

November
ADVICE

Flower Garden

In the flower garden nothing is now to be done except to clean off dead stalks and straw up tender roses, vines, etc., and wherever there is time, to dig up and rake the borders, as it will greatly facilitate spring work. All beds where hyacinths or fall bulbs have been plant-ed, had better be covered with rough

litter or leaves to the depth of two or three inches. If short, thoroughly decayed manure can be spared, a good sprinkling spread over the lawn will help it to a finer growth in spring.

Vegetable Garden

All roots that are in the ground and not designed to be left there all winter, must be dug up in [northern] latitudes before the middle of the month, or they may be frozen until spring; onions, spinach, sprouts, cabbage, or lettuce plants that are outside should be covered with two or three inches of leaves, salt hay, or straw, to protect during winter.

—PETER HENDERSON, *GARDENING FOR PLEASURE*

Fruit Garden

In cold sections the hay or straw mulching may be put on during the last of this month. Grape vines and fruit trees generally should be pruned, and if wood of the vine is wanted for cuttings, or scions of fruit trees for grafts, they should be tied in small neat bunches and buried in the ground until spring.

NOVEMBER

Harvest's End

It gladdens the heart to see the barns and the cellars and the garrets, the corn bins and the root-pits, fill up till they swell with fatness at the end of the summer's growth. It is the result of faithful toil and endeavor, and he must be cold indeed who doesn't get ready for a joyful Thanksgiving.

—THE OLD FARMER'S ALMANAC

THANKSGIVING

A Fall Thanksgiving in the Country

The annual festival, which we call Thanksgiving, has had an increasing popularity from its first establishment. For a long period, it was mostly confined to New England; but, although the mode of observance has greatly changed, its public recognition is greatly extended. In time, it may be observed in every state in the union. The ostensible design of it was to render, in the season of autumn, a general and united expression of gratitude…for the fruits of the earth; and in connection with this, a tribute of thanksgiving for health, civil and religious liberty, and for every kind of prosperity.

—JOHN L. BLAKE, D. D., *THE FARMER'S EVERYDAY BOOK*

Observances

Do not attempt to eulogize your dishes, apologize that you cannot recommend them this is in extreme bad taste; as also the vau ing of the excellence of your wines, etc., et

Do not insist upon your guests partak of particular dishes. Do not ask a pers more than once, and never force a s ply upon their plates.

—MRS. F. L. GILLETTE, *THE WHITE HOUSE COOK BOOK*

FRUIT TRIFLE

hites of four eggs beaten to a stiff froth, two tablespoons
ch of sugar, currant jelly and raspberry jam. Eaten with
onge cakes, it is a delicious dessert.

CRANBERRY SAUCE

ne quart of cranberries, two cupfuls of sugar and a pint
water. Wash the cranberries, then put them on the fire
th the water, but in a covered saucepan. Let them sim-
er until each cranberry bursts open; then remove the
ver of the saucepan, add the sugar and let them all boil
enty minutes without the cover. The cranberries must
ver be stirred from the time they are placed on the fire.
nis is an unfailing recipe for a most delicious preparation
cranberries. Very fine with turkey and game.

CREAMED PARSNIPS

il tender, scrape and slice lengthwise. Put over the fire
th two tablespoonfuls of butter, pepper and salt, and a
le minced parsley. Shake until the mixture boils. Dish
e parsnips, add to the sauce three tablespoonfuls of
eam or milk in which has been stirred a quarter of a
oonful of flour. Boil once and pour over the parsnips.

—MRS. F. L. GILLETTE, *THE WHITE HOUSE COOK BOOK*

Pumpkins are still grown in many gardens with a tenacity that is astonish-
ing, when it should long ago have been known that they have no business
there, as their first cousins, the squashes, are eminently superior for every
culinary purpose whatever. The pumpkin is a valuable product for the farm, as a
food for cattle, but for nothing else. If people will waste valuable land in raising
pumpkins, they may plant them the same as directed for squashes.

—PETER HENDERSON, *GARDENING FOR PLEASURE*

PUMPKIN FOR PIES

Cut up in several pieces, do not pare it; place them on baking tins and set them in
the oven; bake slowly until soft, then take them out, scrape all the pumpkin from
the shell, rub it through a colander. It will be fine and light and free from lumps.

For three pumpkin pies: One quart of milk, three cupfuls of boiled and strained
pumpkin, one and one-half cupfuls of sugar, one-half cupful of molasses, the
yolks and whites of four eggs beaten separately, a little salt, one tablespoonful
each of ginger and cinnamon. Beat all together and bake with an undercrust.

—MRS. F. L. GILLETTE, *THE WHITE HOUSE COOK BOOK*

Best Wishes for Thanksgiving Day.

November is the time to close up the fall work and get ready to go into winter …I always like to plough all I can in the fall…To turn over the land just before it freezes up gives it the best chance to "weather," as they say, so as to crumble down fine and mellow next May.

—THE OLD FARMER'S ALMANAC

CARROTS

~ Carrot salve for blisters: Scrape two carrots and stew in two tablespoons hog's lard. Add two plantain leaves. When the carrots are well done, strain.

—MRS. E. I., IN M. C. TYREE, *HOUSEKEEPING IN OLD VIRGINIA*

~ Carrots are said to improve the eyesight and relieve asthma and rheumatism.

—TRADITIONAL

~ Carrots may be drawn for the table as soon as large enough; but the main crop for storing should not be taken up till quite the end of October, or even later, unless severe frost sets in.

—BEETON'S NEW DICTIONARY OF EVERY-DAY GARDENING

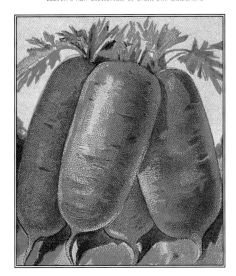

CARROTS FOR COFFEE

The *Prairie Farmer* gives the following recipe for making coffee from carrots. Wash and scrape; then cut in pieces the size of a half an inch square; then dry on a stove. Parch and grind like coffee; or mix equal portions of carrots and coffee as usual. It makes a good drink, and is used by many German emigrants, who say that in their native country there are large factories, where it is packed in paper and sold.

—JOHN L. BLAKE, D. D., *THE FARMER'S EVERYDAY BOOK*

When grass is dry in morning light,
Look for rain before the night,
When dew is on the grass,
Rain will never come to pass.

—·•·—

Weather Wisdom the Year 'Round

Rain before seven, quits before eleven.
Rain long foretold, long last,
Short notice, soon past.

~ If it frosts before November 23rd, it will be a bad winter. ~ If the sun comes out when it's raining, it will rain the next day. ~ An evening gray and morning red,/Will send the shepherd wet to bed. ~ A busy spider lets you know that the weather for the day will be fair, whereas spiders that hide warn us of impending storms. ~ Watch the birds for a daily weather report; if they stop singing, or huddle together with feathers fluffed, a storm is most certainly on its way. ~ If crows can't be easily shooed from the corn field, the coming winter will be a harsh one. ~ The earthworms will come up from underground to greet the coming rain. ~ Do business with men when the wind is from the northwest.

—TRADITIONAL

RECIPES

DECEMBER

To wish you a very MERRY CHRISTMAS

A GREEN CHRISTMAS
MEANS A WHITE EASTER.

December

ADVICE

Flower Garden

We are now fairly into winter, and close attention must be given to protecting all tender plants. There is no rule but vigilance, and as extra strong fires will be kept up, look out again nightly for all combustible matter near the flue or chimney.

Fruit Garden

Grape-vines, raspberries, etc., in sections where protection from severe frost is of advantage, should be attended to this month, by laying them down as near the ground as possible, and covering them with rough litter or leaves, or with a few inches of soil.

Vegetable Garden

Manure and compost heaps should now be forwarded as rapidly as possible, and turned and mixed so as to be in proper condition for spring. Snow that accumulates on cold frames or other glass covers, should be removed, particularly if the soil that the glass covers was not frozen before the snow fell.

—PETER HENDERSON, *GARDENING FOR PLEASURE*

DECEMBER

_____
_____
_____
_____
_____
_____
_____
_____
_____
_____
_____
_____
_____
_____
_____
_____
_____
_____
_____
_____

To Cultivate Poinsettia

Place it in winter quarters before the weather has become cold
enough to chill it, not later than October 1st, as it is a tender
tropical plant, and requires a hot-house temperature of 65° at
night for its full development. Grown in this heat, the bracts
or leaves surrounding the flower clusters average one foot in
diameter; it is in full perfection at the holidays, and is now
largely used for decoration.

—PETER HENDERSON, _PRACTICAL HORTICULTURE_

On Christmas Day

Make a feeding place for
the birds where you can
watch them all the rest of
the winter. They eat garden
insects and weed seeds.
Besides, it's fun.

—THE GARDEN MAGAZINE

Intimate Christmas Presents

If you want to give a garden
loving friend something which
could not possibly be for anyone
else, send one package of your
choicest home-saved seed, with
full directions for cultivation.

Choose the six best recipes
cooking vegetables or preserving
fruits that have been in your fam
for generations, make a booklet
them, and send to the person w
would appreciate them the most

Has your wife enough vases
for cut flowers?

What about a sun dial for
the garden?

Buy a book that will help
someone make a better garden.

—THE GARDEN MAGAZINE

Bell Glass or Cloche

This appliance is much used by gardeners for the protection and culture of lettuces and small vegetables of this character during winter and early spring...It is usually made of ~~gr~~enish glass, and may be had in various sizes, ~~larg~~e enough, in fact, to cover a cauliflower.

—BEETON'S NEW DICTIONARY OF EVERY-DAY GARDENING

Holiday Plants

Holly The custom of decorating with holly at Christmas time is an old one, probably dating from ancient Roman times when holly, considered an emblem of goodwill, was offered at the festival of Saturn.

Mistletoe A few centuries ago, its branches were carried about from house to house, on the first day of January, by young men and maidens, as a new year's gift of friendship.

—MARY PIRIE, A POPULAR BOOK ON FLOWERS, GRASSES AND SHRUBS

A happy CHRISTMAS

~ DECEMBER LORE ~

~ If Christmas comes during a waxing moon, a ~~go~~od year will follow; if Christmas comes during a ~~wa~~ning moon, a hard year will ensue. ~ If the ~~sun~~ shines through the apple boughs on Christmas ~~da~~y, a fine blossoming will ensue; if it's cloudy, ~~tre~~es might die. ~ Many holly berries foretell a ~~har~~d winter.

—TRADITIONAL

A Small Conservatory

There was great rejoicing when the "garden room," as I love to call it, was completed, for it was my winter garden, and I unconsciously gravitated toward it many times a day. The flowers throve beautifully, we raised radishes in February, lettuce in March, and pansy and tomato plants ready to set out when spring opened.

—EDITH L. FULLERTON, *THE GARDEN MAGAZINE*

GREEN THOUGHTS

POTTING

Potting is delightful work. There is nothing better for overwrought nerves than fifteen minutes or half an hour of having one's fingers in the cool, rich earth...To repot a plant set the pot on the bench, place your left hand on the soil, letting the plant stem slip between the index and the middle fingers, then lift the pot in the right hand, turn it upside down, plant and all, and bring the rim of the pot down with a sharp rap on the edge of the bench or table, and the pot can then be lifted off with the right hand, while the plant remains in your left. Pick out, if you can do so without injuring the roots, any of the old drainage material embedded in the roots at the bottom, and fill the hole with fresh soil—this the roots will find more palatable.

—FRANCES DUNCAN, *LADIES' HOME JOURNAL*

This is the end of my vegetable story...We do not pose as professional market gardeners nor as experts; our adventures have merely been those of the average garden lover. There are several marked advantages to be gained from possessing, planting and caring for a garden of one's own. First and foremost is the intimate acquaintance with Mother Nature, which must be ever ennobling, uplifting and broadening; secondly, a freshness and a quality in one's food that is utterly unobtainable through any other source of supply; thirdly a gain in health, if that be needed; and last, but not least, the development of ingenuity, good sense and patience.

—EDITH L. FULLERTON,
HOW TO MAKE A VEGETABLE GARDEN

 ## Labor's Reward

Why is our food so sweet?
Because we earn before we eat.
Why are our wants so very few?
Because we Nature's calls pursue.

—*THE FARMER'S EVERYDAY BOOK*

HOUSEHOLD HINTS

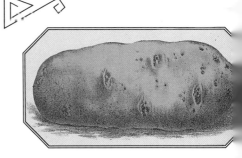

STANDARD SEEDS.

N·O·T·E·S

- To clean mud stains from black cloth dresses, rub with a slice of raw potato.

- To clean knives that have fruit or vinegar stains, rub after washing them with a freshly cut raw potato.

- Stained flower glasses are best cleaned in this way: Put a little vinegar in a glass and add to it a dessert spoonful of soap powder. Shake till all stain is removed, then rinse with warm water.

- Mice dislike mint...Scatter it about the storeroom and you will soon be rid of these tiresome little creatures.

- Ripe tomato will remove inkstains from white cloth or hands.

- Fruit stains can be cleaned from cotton or woolen materials with ammonia and water.

REMEDIES

A cure for nervous headache is to shred a little horseradish and hold it in the palm of the hand until warm. Then snuff it energetically.

For cold and headache take a hot mustard bath.

For burns and scalds, raw onions pounded, or better, scraped and applied as a poultice, give great ease and seem to draw out the "fire."

A poultice of lettuce is calming and very beneficial to anyone suffering from insomnia.

Children often suffer from earaches. An old-fashioned and excellent remedy is to take the heart of an onion (well-baked) and place it in the ear. The effect is most soothing, and will often cause the child to fall asleep when rest before was an impossibility.

HENRY'S HOUSEHOLD COMPANION

COMPLIMENTS OF JOHN F. HENRY & CO. 24 COLLEGE PLACE, NEW YORK

Ink for Garden Use

Dissolve five grains of chloride of platinum in one ounce of distilled water. When dissolved this is ready for use. Keep the mixture tightly corked and use a quill pen when writing.

—MRS. CAMERON LUCY,

Heritage Seed
SUPPLIERS

Abundant Life Seed
  Foundation
P.O. Box 772
Port Townsend, WA 98368
(300) 385-5000

Ambergate Gardens
8015 Krey Avenue
Waconia, MN 55387
(612) 443-2248

Kurt Bluemel, Inc.
2740 Greene Lane
Baldwin, MD 21013
(410) 557-7229

Bluestone Perrenials, Inc.
7211 Middle Ridge Road
Madison, OH 44057
(216) 428-7535

W. Atlee Burpee Company
300 Park Avenue
Warminster, PA 18974
(215) 674-4900

Caprilands Herb Farm
Silver Street
Coventry, CT 06238
(203) 742-7244

Comstock, Ferre, and
  Company
263 Main Street
P.O. Box 125
Wethersfield, CT 06109
(203) 529-3319

Crownsville Nursery
1241 Generalsway Highway
Crownsville, MD 21032
(410) 923-2212

Farmer Seed and
  Nursery Company
818 NW 4th Street
Faribault, MN 55021
(507) 334-1625

Garden Place
6776 Heisley Road
Mentor, OH 44060
(216) 255-3705

Gurney's Seed and
  Nursery Company
110 Capitol Street
Yankton, SD 57079
(605) 665-1671

Heirloom Garden
  Seeds
P.O. Box 138
Guerneville, CA 95446
(707) 869-0967

Henry Field Seed and
  Nursery Company
415 North Burnett
Shenandoah, IA 51601
(712) 246-2011

Hilltop Herb Farm
P.O. Box 1734
Cleveland, TX 77327
(713) 592-5859

Johnny's Selected
  Seeds
Foss Hill Road
Albion, ME 04910
(207) 437-4301

Karutz Greenhouses
1408 Sunset Drive
Vista, CA 92083
(619) 941-3613

Lamb Nurseries
East 101 Sharp Avenue
Spokane, WA 99202
(509) 328-7956

Logee's Greenhouses
141 North Street
Danielson, CT 06239
(203) 774-8038

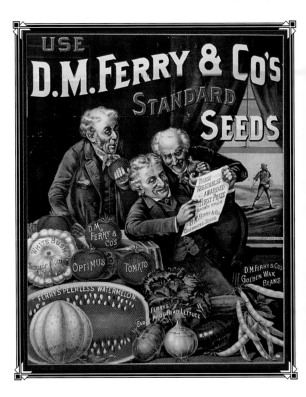

Merry Gardens
P.O. Box 595
Camden, ME 04843
(207) 236-9064

New England Wild
  Flower Society
Garden in the Woods
180 Hemenway Road
Framingham, MA 01701
(508) 877-7630

Nichols Garden
  Nursery
1190 Pacific Highway NE
Albany, OR 97321
(503) 928-9280

Park Seed Company
Cokesbury Road
Greenwood, SC 29647
(803) 223-8555

Perennial Pleasures
  Nursery
2 Brickhouse Road
East Hardwick, VT 05836
(802) 472-5104

Redwood City Seed
  Company
P.O. Box 361
Redwood City, CA 94064
(415) 325-7333

Select Seeds
180 Stickney Hill Road
Union, CT 06076
(203) 684-5655

Shepherd's Garden
Seeds
6116 Highway 9
Felton, CA 95018
(408) 335-5400

Siskiyou Rare Plant
Nursery
2825 Cummings Road
Medford, OR 97501
(503) 772-6846

Southern
Exposure Seed
Exchange
P.O. Box 170
Earlysville, VA
22936
(804) 973-4703

Stokes Seeds, Inc.
P.O. Box 548
Buffalo, NY 14240
(416) 688-4300

Taylor's Herb
Gardens
1535 Lone Oak Rd.
Vista, CA
92084
(619) 727-3485

Thomas Jefferson
Center for
Historic Plants
Monticello
P.O. Box 316
Charlottesville, VA
22902
(804) 979-5283

Vermont Bean Seed
Company
Garden Lane
Fair Haven, VT 05743
(802) 273-3400

Well-Sweep Herb Farm
205 Mount Bethel Road
Port Murray, NJ 07865
(908) 852-5390

White Swan Specialty
Seed Gardens
8030 SW Nimbus Ave.
Beaverton, OR 97005
(503) 641-4477

PICTURE AND TEXT CREDITS

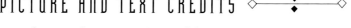

Pictures: The following gave permission for material to be used (c=center, l=left, r=right, t=top, b=bottom, tl=top left, tr=top right, bl=bottom left, br=bottom right.)

Advance Seed Co.: Frontispiece, 26, 46, 50(r), 52(l), 52(r), 95, 124(l), 126, back cover

Marilyn Blaisdell Collection: 64(bl)

Boston Anthenaeum: 91

Angela Burke Coon: 20(tl), 20(bl)

Ethel Z. Bailey Catalogue Collection, L. H. Bailey Hortorium, Cornell University: 35(l), 58(r), 79, 88(b), 106, 118(b)

Fine Art Photographic Library Ltd., London: *A Day in the Garden,* Marian Chase, 36; *A Summer Afternoon,* Frank Walton, 74(b); *Waiting on the Verandah,* Marie Firmin Garard, 102; *A Tea Party in the Garden,* Alfred Oliver, 105(t); *Christmas Cheer,* George Sheridan Knowls, 116; *Christmas Fruit and Nuts,* Eloise Harriette Stannard, 120(l); *A Bright and Happy Christmas,* Anonymous, 120(r)

Lyon's Antique Prints: 45(b), 47, 58(b), 98(b), 108(b), 110(t), 111(t), 127(b)

Jan Hughes Collection: 5, 7, 8(tl), 8(r), 9(t), 9(b), 14(tl), 14(tr), 14(c), 15, 18, 19, 21, 25, 32, 34(b), 35(r), 38(l), 38(r), 39, 40–41(b), 49, 55, 58(l), 59(b), 60(l), 61(tl), 61(r), 62(t), 62(b), 68(l), 71(l), 75, 78(l), 78(r), 78(b), 80(t), 82, 83(l), 87, 88(l), 88(r), 89, 92(l), 92(b), 94, 98(l), 99, 104(r), 108(l), 109, 110(b), 112, 113(l), 117, 118(l), 119, 121(bl), 123(l), 127(t)

Courtesy of the National Agricultural Library, Special Collections: 13, 17, 28(l), 51(r), 56, 85, 123(r)

Northwind Picture Archives: 10(bl), 53

Courtesy of the San Francisco Public Library: 8(bl), 20(r), 30(br), 33(r), 34(t), 48(b), 73(tl), 81(r), 100(r), 103(r), 124(l)

Smithsonian Institution, Archives Center, National Museum of American History, Warshaw Collection: 10(t), 28(r), 48(r), 65, 66–67, 68(r), 76, 98(r), 108(r), 111(b), 118(r), 122, 125(r)

Allison C, Smith: 44(b)

Nursery Catalogue Collection, Department of Special Collections, University of California, Davis: front, 3, 6, 11(l), 11(r), 12, 14(b), 16, 22(r), 27, 29, 30(tl), 30(tr), 30(bl), 31(l), 31(r), 33(l), 37, 38(b), 40(tl), 40(bl), 41(t), 42(l), 42(r), 43, 45(tl), 48(l), 50(l), 51(l), 57, 59(t), 60(r), 63, 64(tr), 69, 70, 71(r), 72, 77, 80(l), 80(br), 83(r), 86, 90(l), 90(r), 92(r), 93, 96, 97, 100(l), 101(l), 101(r), 104(l), 107, 121(br), 128

Text: All month-opener quotes are traditional sayings drawn from *The Perpetual Almanack of Folklore,* by Charles Knightly [London: Thames and Hudson, 1994], and *The Country Diary of an Edwardian Lady,* by Elizabeth Holden [London: Michael Joseph/Webb & Bower, 1977].

HORTICULTURAL BOOKS

BIBLIOGRAPHY

Bailey, L. H. *Garden-Making,* 8th ed. New York: The Macmillan Co., 1904.

Beecher, Henry Ward. *Pleasant Talk about Fruits, Flowers and Farming.* New York: J. B. Ford & Co., 1874.

Beeton's Dictionary of Every-Day Gardening. London: Ward, Lock & Co., Ltd., 1861.

Blake, John L. *The Farmer's Everyday Book.* Auburn, NY: Derby & Miller, 1850.

Ely, Helena Rutherfurd. *A Woman's Hardy Garden.* New York: The Macmillan Co., 1903.

Fullerton, Edith L. *How To Make a Vegetable Garden.* New York: Doubleday Page & Co., 1905.

Gillette, Mrs. F. L. *The White House Cook Book.* New York: Saalfield Publishing Co., 1887.

Haines, Jennie Day, ed. *De Gardenne Boke.* San Francisco: Paul Elder & Co., 1906.

Henderson, Peter. *Gardening for Pleasure.* New York: Orange Judd Co., 1886.

——. *Practical Horticulture.* New York: Orange Judd Co., 1889.

Lucy, Mrs. Cameron. *Hearts and Spades.* London: J. Ouseley, Ltd., 1911.

Pirie, Mary. *A Popular Book on Flowers, Grasses, & Shrubs.* London: James Blackwood & Co., [N. D.].

Sylvester, Charles H., ed. *Journeys Through Bookland.* Chicago: Bellows-Reeve Company, 1909.

Thaxter, Celia. *An Island Garden.* Boston: Houghton Mifflin, 1894.

Thoreau, Henry David. *Walden, or Life in the Woods.* Boston: James R. Osgood & Co., 1854.

Tyree, Marion Cabell. *Housekeeping in Old Virginia.* Louisville, KY: John P. Morton & Co., 1879.

Warner, Charles Dudley. *My Summer in a Garden.* Boston: James R. Osgood & Co., 1878.

Other sources include: *Atlanta:* May 1893 (33); *Cornhill Magazine:* January 1903 (33); *Country Life in America:* May 1905 (90), July 1905 (20), June 1907 (94); *The Delineator:* March 1909 (14, 25); *D. M. Ferry Descriptive Catalogue:* 1876 (30); *The Garden Magazine:* August 1905 (83), September 1905 (94), December 1905 (61, 120, 122), January 1906 (10); *The Independent:* October 1909 (34); *Ladies' Home Journal:* January 1907 (9), February 1907 (70), March 1907 (28, 30), April 1907 (11, 39), May 1907 (82, 115), June 1907 (45, 85), August 1907 (81), June 1908 (62, 123); *The Living Age:* April 27 1907 (41, 64, 73); *The Old Farmer's Almanac:* May 1821 (51), September 1842 (100), November 1872 (109); *The Outing Magazine:* March 1908 (71), November 1908 (103); *Review of Reviews:* July 1893 (44); *Shaker Seed Catalogue:* 1873 (21).

ACKNOWLEDGMENTS

The editors and publishers would like to thank the following for their invaluable help with the preparation of this book: John Scarsdat, Head of Shields Library Special Collections, University of California, Davis; Victoria Yturralde, Shields Library Special Collections, University of California, Davis; Samuel Woo, Medical Illustrations, University of California, Davis; Sherry J. Vance, L.H.B. Hortorium, Cornell University; Judy Ho, Special Collections, National Agricultural Library; Dennis Bixler, Vice President of the Development for the Associates of the National Agricultural Library; Marvin Mitchell, The Balliol Corporation; John Hamrick, Advance Seed Company; Ada Fitzsimmons; Shelagh Ross; Sharon Marks; Tracy Ginther; Jeff Holland and Nick Baklanoff.